UNDER

TRUE STORIES
OF OVERCOMING ADVERSITY

SCOTT KUJAK

Revival Enterprises LLC

This book is dedicated to my good friend, Phil Taylor,
and the entire Taylor family

Table of Contents

Yet before all these things: under

How anyone moves up?

It is quite a wonder

That anyone can accomplish

Anything at all

Too skinny to be mighty

Too short to ball

Too little of something

And well below average

Makes one too fearless to quit

And all that more savage

Too many times, told "no"

Too often rejected

Underlie all the people

Adored and respected

The Underdog

PEOPLE LOVE TO cheer for the underdog. Unless the spectator is a diehard fan for a specific team, most people elect to cheer for the underdog in a major sporting competition because they want to see that team beat the odds. Everyone in life has been told by a doubter that a goal they have in life would be unattainable. Most people know the joyful fulfillment of proving the doubter wrong after they have accomplished the goal. We are drawn to the underdog stories in society, careers, sports, and relationships, because, in them, we see a reflection of the belief in ourselves. We cherish the underdog who comes out on top. Their tenacious characteristics are what we strive to obtain.

It has been a tremendous honor to capture the stories of numerous people who have overcome adversity. This book is a result of the Underdog Podcast. On the show, I interview underdogs who beat the odds and learned a wiser perspective on life by going through their own adversity. The following chapters contain ten stories from the first forty episodes of the podcast. Each story is separate and stands on its own, but the recurring theme in all ten stories is the spirit of the fight against their adversity to pursue their goals. They all fought against their adversity in a unique manner and won in the end in their own way.

The podcast began when I witnessed my good friend battle cancer at a young age. I was living in Southern California completing my training program for my career (I live in Austin, Texas now), and I was in the midst of the most difficult time of my life. I was inspired by the way my friend responded to his fight against cancer because his reactions were often much different than mine. His faith, optimism, and selflessness helped me reexamine my position, and I strived to act more like him. Since he had such an impact on me, I searched for a way to broadcast his message to more people, including strangers, and the idea for the podcast was born.

I had an extremely difficult time selecting the ten stories because I could have easily written a chapter for each episode. Every interview contained drama, significance, wonder, wisdom, teaching, healing, and an inspiring perspective in their own unique way. I do not get an opportunity to meet most of the people that I interview, so some of these interviews contain just the guest's story without my presence in the story, while other chapters include interactions from my personal relationship with them.

I would like to thank all of the amazing guests from the podcast for sharing their stories with us. The following ten stories are not ranked in any specific order as it is impossible to rank these underdogs. I try to provide various stories of underdogs who overcame unforeseen circumstances that were out of their control, and also, people whose self-imposed decisions provided the means for them to become an underdog in a new setting.

I used the interview with each guest as my guide to each chapter. Any time sentences are in italicized font, then those words are a direct quote taken from the podcast interview of the guest. The back of the book contains an archive of the guests from the first forty episodes, and a brief summary of their story. You can find more information at www.underdogpc.com as well.

My hope is that you will be inspired, and that at least one of these stories, if not all of them, will change your outlook on life forever. We cannot necessarily relate to every situation from every single person, but we can relate to the feelings of hopelessness and despair that comes from pain and brokenness. We can choose to empathize with anyone. I pray that the next time you face your own obstacles that you embrace the underdog mentality and choose to fight against adversity with courage, strength, precision, and patience just like these guests did. Discover the fighting underdog spirit within you and unleash it.

CHAPTER 1

Episode 18 – Unshattered After Sepsis

Carol Decker

Arrival

"I relearned how to do everything again from walking and eating, to being a mom and a wife."

"Push! C'mon you're doing great! Keep going! Push!" yells the doctor. Monitors blink, nurses hurry to and fro, and mom lets out a howl of pain.

Finally with one last "Push!" call from the doctor and one last groan from mom, the new baby girl arrives into the world and the room is filled with the baby's cry. The world has gained another miracle. Mom endured hours of excruciating pain, and she starts to ease her tension. Mom has made it through all of the cravings, back aches, sleepless nights, book-reading, baby showers, crib-building, and anxiety of the past nine months. Her world has officially changed forever. There is no going back.

Patiently awaiting the arrival of a newborn is perhaps the most anxious and exciting time of life for a young mother. Nine months of preparation seems like an eternity during the suspense.

Childbirth in the United States tends to be a safe process for the mother and child due to the highest quality healthcare in the world. It is unusual for a mother or child to suffer severe complications during birth in the land of the free and the brave.

The pain of childbirth for mom results in the most satisfying and perfect gift. There could not be a moment to look back more fondly on in life, than this.

When Carol Decker entered the emergency room with flu-like symptoms, the doctors told her that she needed to have an emergency C-section immediately. When Carol woke up, she was permanently blind, and the blindness was the first of many irreversible changes that she experienced. She had the first opportunity to hold her baby girl multiple days after her birth, and she was in a tremendous amount of pain when she did. Her life as she once knew it, would never be the same.

Enumclaw, Washington State

Carol is a Washington State native. She was born in Kennewick and grew up with older brothers who constantly tested her competitive spirit in her favorite passion, snowboarding. Some of her fondest memories from childhood involved steep mountains and top speeds cutting through the icy air and racing against her brothers. She went to BYU-Idaho and met her husband, Scott, when she was a sophomore. They married in 1998 and eventually settled in Enumclaw, Washington in 2006 which is about an hour southeast of Seattle.

Scott and Carol were blessed with the conception of a second child a short time after the birth of their first daughter, Chloe. Both were filled with excitement to bring a second blessing into the world. Scott's dental practice was operating smoothly. Chloe's growth was on track with other infants her age. The bills were paid. Life was good. Another family member would only bring more bliss to this happy family in the quiet town of Enumclaw.

On June 10, 2008, she was rushed to the hospital because her flu-like symptoms were becoming more and more severe. The doctors informed her and Scott after initial tests and examinations that they needed to perform an emergency C-section. This was scary news. The nurses and aides pushed Carol, lying on a gurney, to the surgery room. Scott walked by her side, and clasped her trembling hand. They were fearful of the uncertainty that lay ahead, but they had faith. Their hands slipped apart after one last squeeze, and they both said, "Goodbye."

That final moment in the gurney on the way to surgery was the last time that she ever physically saw the person she loves most on this earth. She woke up in complete darkness and was never again able to leave the darkness behind. She had become permanently blind. Three of her limbs were amputated a couple of weeks after her daughter's birth. Both of her legs were lost from the knees down. A blood clot later formed in her left wrist, and she lost her left hand. Finally, the hospital staff removed her right ring finger, but she fortunately kept her right hand. Her body's sensory awareness and life functionality changed forever. And, most crucially, she was still fighting to stay alive.

Sepsis was the culprit. Sepsis is the body's overwhelming and life-threatening response to infection which can lead to tissue damage, organ failure, and death. It claims over 258,000 lives each year in the United States and is the third leading cause of death. This malady carries a 25-30% mortality rate and kills more individuals than prostate cancer, breast cancer, and HIV/AIDS combined. It is the number one cost of hospitalization in the U.S., and antibiotic administration decreases the likelihood of death by 7.6% per hour. Diagnosing and treating sepsis as quickly as possible is of the utmost significance (Center for Disease Control. www.cdc.gov).

"My feet and hands turned black in different parts of my body. I had blood clots all over my body and skin grafting on thirty percent of my body. Skin grafts are literally the most excruciating, horrific pain that I have ever gone through in my entire life. And, at the time, I didn't know I was blind either."

Strep pneumonia bacteria infected her blood stream and caused her body to undergo septic shock. The infection and resulting immune response attempted to attack everything in her body including her ocular nerves which is why she became blind. She fought for her life for three months, confined to the hospital. After the three months, Carol, very much alive, got to journey home with her new daughter, Safiya, who was healthy and full of life.

Relearning How to Live

Her journey to full recovery began the moment she entered the hospital, and it lasted for a much longer time after those initial three months. Most patients are filled with joyful enthusiasm when the doctor releases them to return home. But, then again, most patients return home to a normal life.

"I thought that it would be really exciting to go home, but when I went home I realized that my husband would have to help me onto the toilet and then into my bed, because I was in a state that I couldn't do anything for myself. I was like a newborn infant myself."

Returning home to the last place where she had a memory of a "normal" life and had been anxiously awaiting the birth of her new baby girl was a cruel plot twist when she finally arrived there even though she already knew her life was changed forever. Being in her house triggered the reminder of her own losses, and it served as the reminder that she would not be able to take care of her husband, nor Chloe, nor her new baby girl. Carol and Safiya required the same amount of effort and attentiveness from her husband and family, and the only difference was that Carol could speak.

"And as my pain started to increase and my anxiety started to become uncontrollable, the first thing I told my husband when I got home is that he needed to take me back to the hospital, that I didn't belong here, that I couldn't take care of my kids, and that he couldn't take care of me. It was really difficult. That reality of coming home was really hard for me. I knew that at that point I needed to make a choice whether I would work harder than I ever have to get the life

back that I had before, or if I was just going to give up. At the time when I was going through that I was in a really deep, dark depression. It was really hard to make those choices, but the one thing that got me through the depression was my support system."

Fortunately, Carol's friends, family, and even the community rallied around her. Her husband showed his dedication to her by standing by her side during her fight to restart her life. Her family set up a blog to update everyone else on the status of her recovery and donations poured in to help the family with the medical bills. We have all heard of the African proverb, "It takes a village to raise a child," and the people of Enumclaw, Washington stepped up to the challenge to raise this family back up on to their feet. This community effort was the driving force that pushed back against her depression.

Cookies, High Heels, and Snowboarding

Her recovery was slow, frustrating, and painful while she relearned how to perform daily tasks again. However, it was a necessary process for her body to have the opportunity to heal and for her spirit to recover as well. She discovered that through goal setting she broke down the wall of depression one brick at a time that surrounded her. Yet, her determination did not originate from a desire to regain motor functions for personal use, instead, it stemmed from relearning how to accomplish motherly tasks for her girls.

"For me, it was being a mom again. I couldn't hold Safiya because it hurt so bad to hold her. My hand didn't work so I couldn't take care of her. So, the therapist found ways to motivate me to become a mom again. I told my brother, Heath, that I would never be able to make cookies with my daughters again."

Her deepest grief came from the fear that she would miss the mother-daughter moments she so wished to cherish as her babies grew up. Her support system rallied and set the ball in motion to help her break through her own sense of mental limitations.

"One day my family's caretaker brought in some cookie dough

and said, 'Were going to make cookies today.' And I said, 'No, I can't do it.' And she said, 'Nope we're going to.' Chloe and I started rolling out the dough and Safiya was pounding the dough on the table because she was just a baby. Then Chloe tapped my nose with her fingers filled with flour and in that moment this window of opportunity opened. I was doing something with my children that I never thought possible. There were many more opportunities to come, I just had to look at things in a different way."

The cloud of darkness began to dissipate more and more each time she accomplished a new goal because she didn't stop with just baking cookies. When Carol and her doctors were preparing to fit her for prosthetic legs she created a goal that blew the doctors' minds. She had a stretch goal to wear her high heels and walk into her favorite restaurant in Seattle using her prosthetics the following year for her birthday. The doctor initially told her that it was a great goal to set, but she later discovered through a friendship that formed with this doctor that she thought Carol was setting an absurd goal for herself. Carol proved it to herself and to many others that she was going to put her money where her mouth was. On August 7, 2009, she had dinner with her family and friends at that restaurant, and she walked in and out of that restaurant wearing her favorite pair of high heels.

"That was huge to me. No one in the restaurant had any idea that the year before I was fighting for my life in the hospital."

Some goals hold a deeper significance than others. It is difficult to imagine a goal with more profound ingredients than one that combines a childhood passion with family bonding. She grew up on the mountainside ripping through fresh-powdered snow on her snowboard. Her best childhood memories are filled with competitive races down the slopes against her brothers.

"When Safiya turned five, I set a goal that I would go up to the mountain and ski or snowboard with them."

Carol was connected with the "Outdoors for All" organization through some of her friends. Their mission is "to enrich the quality of life for children and adults with disabilities through outdoor recreation." She shined with the opportunity she was given, and one of her most desired wishes became a near-and-dear treasure in her heart.

She took an eight-week course in January 2014, and learned how to ski on a "sit-ski." One time, she remembers some of the guys from "Outdoors for All" trying to help her get on the chairlift. While they were picking her up, the back of the chairlift hit the back of her skis and she fell down on top of her head. While some people would get upset, she laughed! The guys were really nervous and silent, but Carol just said, *"Pretty much the worst thing that could have happened just did. So, we got that out of the way and let's go have some fun."*

"A month later, in February 2014, I went up with my family for the first time, and we skied together as a family. It was literally one of the best moments of my life as I listened to my daughter ski by and say, 'Hi mommy!' I carved back and forth in the fresh powder, and of course, I fell. After I fell in the snow, the guys came over to ask if I was okay, and, in that moment, I just stopped and said, 'Yes, give me a minute. I want to lie here.' To be there five years later at my favorite place … I just felt like I could have died and gone to heaven."

Carol relearned how to live life to the fullest, one moment at a time. She may not be able to roll the cookie dough into perfect circles by herself but that doesn't mean she cannot soak in her daughters' laughter while they try. She can't wiggle her toes, but she can still wipe the dust off her favorite pair of heels and strut into her favorite restaurant. And, she won't be able to rip through fresh powder like she once did, but she can still enjoy the cold snow enough to lay in it and be satisfied with peace on the top of a mountain with her family. She found the will to never give up. She found a new appreciation for life.

Las Vegas

I met Carol because she came to speak at my company's national sales meeting in Las Vegas in early 2018. I work for a well-known medical device company that manufactures and distributes laboratory diagnostic capital equipment for hospitals around the world. A person's blood is drawn into a test tube and then that test tube is sent down to the hospital lab. The test tubes are placed on instruments that take a sample of the blood and test it to get an accurate red blood cell and white blood cell count. The instruments also detect the presence of abnormal cells such as proliferating white blood cells and the data is given in a report. The report helps the physician determine what the diagnosis is and how to treat the patient moving forward. My company sells those crucial patient care instruments.

There was a lot of buzz around this meeting, because the company had a plan to submit to the United States Food & Drug Administration a new parameter that would aid in the diagnosis of sepsis. So, my company leadership found the perfect guest speaker in Carol to motivate us to sell these new instruments and new features with the hope of decreasing the growing cases of sepsis each year. That evening, her story had a profound impact on me and touched all of the five hundred-plus individuals in attendance. I knew that I had to capture her story on my podcast because of the powerful impression she had just made on every sales associate in the company.

Since that session, I've had the opportunity to reflect on the reasons for doing any sales job. It is so easy for a salesperson to be consumed by quotas, commission dollars, and competition within their own peer group. The big picture becomes fuzzy, and the correct motive wanders off. So many sales agents are driven by making more and more money. The dollar trumps family bonding, authentic relationships, love, volunteering, and time for relaxation. Why is that? For status? For impressions? For false security? It's all a mirage. Many people have witnessed their colleagues ruin their health and relationships in the pursuit of more net worth. It is truly a sad sight to see when greed operates the steering wheel. People correlate their bank account with their self-worth and value to society.

The national sales team had the opportunity to partner with hospitals and provide a new instrument that would save patient lives and help detect sepsis much sooner than any current method on the market. The sales staff has the opportunity to prevent amputations, blindness, and skin grafting to patients who suffer from the results of sepsis such as Carol. That should always be the priority reason for selling and not any of the fancy accolades that come with hitting a quota. Her suffering and her grit hit us harder than any Mike Tyson blow would have if we were inside the ring with him across the street at MGM Grand. Her story put our blessings and opportunities in perspective. It made me and many others re-assess our own intentions in our daily life.

"This could have happened to any of us. This could have happened to me," was what I wrestled with in my mind after the conclusion of her speech. I have taken so many things in life for granted. I have complained about the most insignificant annoyances, because I thought my life was too vigorous to deal with tedious irritations. And yet, Carol lost so much without warning or preparation. She suffered physically and emotionally for years after this unforeseen trial. Most people would have given up because the dream life they lived for in the past was just a distant memory now. She fought against the naysayers and self-doubt. She pushed herself to cherish a new perspective on life. She became forever grateful.

Let Go! Embrace the Moment and Have Fun

Carol is living her life with no regrets. She chooses to live by the motto "Let go, embrace the moment and have fun".

"Let go, means to let go of fear. Anyone will be able to accomplish a lot more of their goals and try new things. This really helped me in the beginning with my therapists. It also means to forgive oneself or forgive the other people that person is blaming because it is such a burden to carry that. The second thing I say is 'embrace the moment'. My own counselor told me that I wasn't able to change the past and that I couldn't go back, but I could make goals for the future. She asked me to start thinking of the moments in my life throughout

the day and embrace these simple moments, such as waking up and hearing my children. And the last thing is to 'have fun,' because life is worth living."

The motto of "Let Go! Embrace the moment and have fun." was on display the first time I scheduled her for an interview. We set a date for early March 2018, and on the day of the interview I was running late. I was at a customer appointment a few hours from my house, and I was trying to fight the Austin, Texas rush hour traffic to get home. I finally arrived home ten minutes before our agreed upon time. I was anxious to get out of my suit and set up my recording equipment, so I rushed through the front door with the stress of poor time management ticking in my ear.

Before I headed upstairs, I walked outside to let my dog, Kaya, in the house. She had been left outside all day. I was in befuddled disbelief. Kaya was not attached to her dog run, although her collar was hanging from it and a couple of fence rails were chewed up and busted in pieces, lying on the ground. Then I peeked over the fence to see that my neighbor's belongings had exploded into tiny pieces as if Major League Baseball Hall of Fame pitcher, Randy Johnson, had thrown a 98 mph fastball grenade in the center of the yard. Kaya was curled up in the corner trying to put on her cutest and best "Please have mercy on me" puppy-dog look. Austin traffic, mixed with running late, mixed with dog mischief had steam coming out of my ears, and I still could not put the pieces of the puzzle together to solve how she got out of her dog run and into my neighbor's yard.

I quickly told Carol that I would be a little late to our appointment and knocked on the neighbor's door and politely said, "My dog got through the fence and ate everything in your yard before returning to the security of my own backyard. Can I fix all of this for you?" He said I could.

I zoomed through the picking-up and told the neighbor that I would replace the missing fence rails later. I finally got to my house and set up my recording equipment and called Carol and told her about the strange happenings at my home. We went through the entire interview, but it must have been like pulling teeth for her. My mind was so frazzled by the chain of events that I struggled formulating my follow-up questions to her responses. A monkey would have sounded like an exquisite Shakespearean king if you contrasted it to my jungle gibberish. At the end, I couldn't live with my performance anymore, and I summoned up the courage to ask her for more of her time on a different day so that my mind could return to a normal human's coherent state. She could have been frustrated with my request, instead she decided to "let go" of my egg-on-the-face performance, "embrace" the opportunity to share her story again at a later date, and "have fun" by laughing off my inability to solve my own Hound of Baskervilles mystery.

She is filled with joy to live life and share her story, and I am so thankful that she graced me with accepting a rescheduled invitation. She was the first person, and the only person I've ever had to reschedule because of hectic events in my life.

And, just so you know, I eventually put two-and-two together and realized that Kaya had jumped onto the dog house which was lined up against the fence. She forgot that she was tied up and attempted to jump into the neighbor's yard which gave her the necessary force to slip out of her collar. With newfound freedom, she decided to have a field day and shred everything in sight. After her adrenaline rush ended, she realized that she was in deep trouble and chewed through the fence rails to soften them up enough before she barreled through them like a running back who pummeled through linebackers on his way to score a touchdown. When she returned to my yard, she hoped that I wouldn't notice the missing rails or the tornado that hit my neighbor's yard because she was calmly lying down in my backyard - so … how could she have caused such a wreckage? I will not share how long it took for me to solve this puzzle out of fear of Sherlock Holmes turning over in his grave in the fiction afterlife.

Life is a Gift

Carol travels all over the country sharing her story and sharing hope and encouragement with others. She is currently on tour for her new book, and she grows in popularity with every life that she touches. She is often asked if she would change what happened to her. That is a deep question, because there are so many unknowns. I don't know how I would respond if it were up to me, but she always responds with the same loving answer.

"I honestly say no because I've had so many amazing opportunities to meet different people and give back by sharing my story. I look at my challenges as a blessing. I see things in such a different way and I'm so grateful for that perspective on my life. I'm grateful that I can get out of bed and be with my kids. I'm glad that I get to feel the sunshine on my face. I want to experience my life in a positive way. I still have days that are tough where I get upset, but some things are out of our control. What we can control is our attitude and how we live our lives. I want to take control over that and choose for myself."

A large reason for that gratitude comes from her husband's unending love. Her husband, Scott, could have easily decided to leave when this all first happened. In a divorce-stricken culture, he could have made any excuse in the book to remove himself as the caretaker of the family but he never had the slightest idea to jump ship. His love and commitment to his family was a stronger foundation than any storm that could rain down on it.

"I love him so much. He is the love of my life. It has been really hard to go through what we went through. Having the patience to get through this has been difficult and stressful on our marriage, but we came through it and fought for the love we have for each other. When someone loves you, it is their choice. He didn't have to do the things that he did or stay by my side. He didn't have to pick me up and carry me to the shower, or do my makeup, or dress me. But he chose to, and I love him more for that." She is Superwoman and we shouldn't overlook the fact that she has Clark Kent by her side.

Carol recently published her book in June 2018, <u>Unshattered: Overcoming Tragedy and Choosing a Beautiful Life</u>, which is her own narrative about her life story. She published it on the ten-year anniversary mark of when sepsis changed her life forever. Her story and her perspective is a gift to anyone she crosses paths with. In her own words, *"Life is a gift. If you don't open it you'll never experience the beauty inside."*

CHAPTER 2

Episode 35 - Burning Ironman

Shay Eskew

Yellow Jackets

My uncle has owned and operated his own pest control business in the Dallas-Fort Worth metropolitan area for over twenty years. He leaves the house every morning before the rooster crows to travel long distances to wherever duty calls. Termites, wasps, fire ants, mosquitoes, snakes, and critters stand no chance against Anderson's Pest Control. However, in a lot of those circumstances, those aggravated pests do not go down without a fight.

My uncle has shared many enthralling stories of pain, panic, and fury. One of his stories even included running around a client's house stripping his clothes off because angry bees found a way to get inside his clothing, and stung him all over his body!

My uncle has been bit and stung by every living creature you can find in North Texas, but his encounters with yellow jackets never burned him like it did for Shay Eskew.

Shay is from Marietta, Georgia, and grew up in the most conservative household that anyone can imagine. Picture the most southern Baptist Church parents that you can think of, and then multiply that by ten, and you will have an idea of what his parents were like. His parents made sure that he avoided danger like the devil learned to avoid Georgia when a young fiddler player named Johnny lived there. So, an eight-year old Shay jumped on the opportunity to warn a neighbor about their aggressive yellow jackets in an underground nest after his mother suggested that he do so. He and his friend, Jeff, met the fifteen-year old neighbor across the street, and agreed to show her the nest after she asked for their assistance. She struck a match and threw it into the underground yellow jacket nest where he and Jeff stood close by making sure that none of the yellow jackets were escaping. The match did nothing, and the boys had no idea what she would do next. Then, without warning, the neighbor threw a cup of gasoline into the hole, and accidentally splashed Shay and Jeff with it. They were immediately engulfed in flames, and their shrieks of torment echoed down the streets.

Push-ups and Sit-ups

Shay immediately stopped-dropped-and-rolled and put his flames out. Then, he grabbed the hose and put out the flames on Jeff.

"I grabbed a hose, put him out, and basically just stood there alternating the hose between us. Finally, one of the other neighbors heard us screaming and contacted my mom, who happened to be home. She ran across the street, and obviously, was just floored looking at us. Portions of our bodies were completely charred, other portions were blackened, and our skin was peeling off. I remember touching my head, and all of my hair came out. Our clothes were melted to our bodies."

An athletic eight-year old boy had become almost unrecognizable in an instant. He spent the next three months in the hospital, and, in addition to the pain and stress of the burn trauma, his family was responsible for a two million dollar hospital bill because his father's company had canceled insurance policies previously on dependents. The ultra-conservative little family living in the suburbs of Atlanta would never know life as it once was, and they needed their faith more than ever.

The doctors amputated his right ear because it became gangrenous. He lost three skin grafts to infection. The harvested skin grafts from the donor sites on his thighs was dug too deep and left his donor sites with the equivalent damage of a third degree burn. The medical team took skin off the back of his legs to fix the original donor sites on the front of his thighs. He was burned on thirty-five percent of his body, but the resulting complications and multiple infections increased the affected and damaged portions of his body to sixty-five percent.

Shay had serious setbacks and challenges. His right arm was melted to his side. His head suffered from a similar web defect and he did not have the ability to hold his head up straight. He needed three years to learn how to hold his head up straight and how to lift his arm over his head. During those three years, he had to wear custom orthotic braces on his face, his neck, and his side, in addition to a pressure fitted garment suit that went from his ankles, to his wrists, and to his neck to minimize the thickening of the scar tissue. He remembers all of this, but what he remembers the most is the doctors telling him that he would most likely never be able to play competitive sports again. The news of the inability to become an athlete hurt him the deepest.

Shay went from being the most athletic kid on every youth sports team to the kid who was picked last at every recess event. And although this new reality of life stung, he did not let his inabilities deter him from his goals. He completed the third grade by relearning how to write left-handed. He played second base for his Little League baseball team two months after his release from the hospital since he could only throw the ball side-armed, and that was the shortest distance to throw to first base. Though a child, he found the will to never give up because he had one dream – become one of the best athletes.

"These scars are never going to get better. I'm going to have these the rest of my life, but I asked myself, 'What can I do to become an athlete?' And so, everything I did was focused on becoming an athlete. When I first went back to school, I went from being one of the

first ones picked to being the last one picked. Nobody wanted me on their team. I was also unfortunate enough that my injuries came at the same time that Wes Craven's movie, 'Nightmare on Elm Street', came out, and I remember walking through the schools and generally I would hear a few people make comments, 'Hey Freddy', as in Freddy Krueger, and, honestly, when I looked in the mirror, that's what I saw."

He became the subject of every whisper in the hallways at school when he was previously quite popular. The long school days were tough for him, and the sleepless nights were even tougher. Sometimes he cried himself to sleep, but even at the age of eight-years-old, he chose to remain confident in his faith. He believed that God had bigger plans for him in the future.

He learned how to be not just physically tough, but emotionally tough. Going from the schoolyard star to riding the bench is an abrupt transition for anyone. The bullying due to his deformities were defeating for his confidence. He had scars on sixty-five percent of his body, and he could not hide all of them. People quickly saw his scars whenever they met him and often judged him for the worse because of it. He had a tough pill to swallow in school, and it only got more difficult during the progression of his thirty-five plus surgeries over the next thirty years.

"In 1982, burn trauma and the treatment, were nowhere near like it is today. We didn't get morphine then. They didn't do induced comas. The strongest thing I ever got for pain meds was extra strength Tylenol before they put me in the tank to scrub me. When they cut off pieces of my ear, most of it was done while I was awake with a pair of scissors. It's kind of hard to fathom now, but it's what made me who I am. It made me impervious to pain. I realized that pain is temporary, and a lot of it's mental. I convinced myself that pain doesn't hurt as bad as I think it may at first."

Debridement, the process of removing dead tissue on a burn wound by scrubbing with gauze and sterile water, is noted by many healthcare professionals as the most painful experience one can endure. Shay underwent it as an eight-year old with only over-the-counter

17

pain medication, and he had the procedure done multiple times. He trained his mind to view the unbearable pain as progression in the necessary development to become an elite athlete.

Most children would have been terrified and cried for hours leading up to surgery knowing the pain that the future held in the operating room. He shocked others with his preparation routine before all of his surgeries while he was in high school and college.

"I knew there was a chance that I may wake up and not have the same mobility I had before the surgery. There's always a risk for potential complications. So, I would exercise in my room doing push-ups, jumping jacks, sit-ups, knowing if I woke up and I couldn't do those same things in the morning, I made use of every minute I had. I had no regrets. I think that's one of the things that's always served me well in life is that I don't assume there's going to be a tomorrow. I pray there will be, but I try to make the most of every day, in every situation, knowing that it is my last time. I never played it safe, and I made use of every second to give everything I had."

Many people struggle to find the determination to work out and push their body to the limit. He continues to treat every day like it may be his last, and it has paid him many dividends.

Women, Wrestling, and Boxing

The quest for love is one that all people embark on during life. It's one of the most terrifying and elating pursuits that one can experience, and the risks are great. Rejection versus companionship are the options that all people face when they search for a relationship. Shay grew up bullied and ostracized, and his scars were visible, so dating was more than difficult for him. Girls were quick to pass him by while he was growing up, yet he knew that sports would tell a different story for him in the long run.

"For the first probably six to eight years, I always made sure I presented my good side of my body first to people. I really thought if I was a good athlete that people would overlook the scars, and I felt

that it was one of those things that at least would force people to give me a second look, or to find out more about who I really am. Sports gave me a great platform. It allowed me to have conversations with girls, and guys, too. Once they really knew what I stood for, the scars became irrelevant. I was fortunate enough that I met my wife when I was in grad school, and she was willing to see beyond the scars. I've never really asked her in detail about it, but it was never really an issue for her."

Shay found love when he met the woman who would become his wife, but he found success as an athlete way before that. Finding a way to level the playing field was an important step in his strategy to prove his worthiness as an athlete. He was too small to play football, and not fast enough to play soccer, so he had to turn to other sports. In high school, he found success in wrestling and boxing where he was evenly matched by weight with his opponent, and he stayed with these sports through college.

He always felt that, pound-for-pound, he could go toe-to-toe with anybody. Wrestling and boxing provided the opportunity to prove himself in this way. He viewed these sports as a competition of which opponent had the highest pain threshold and the greatest endurance ability. All he needed to do to improve was put in the time to develop the skills necessary to refine his competitive advantage.

His boxing and wrestling skills developed quickly. He not only became good in competition, but he became the best. He was a three-time region champion in wrestling in high school, and, as a junior, placed second in the state. Plus, his accolades continued to multiply into adulthood, because he was inducted into the National Wrestling Hall of Fame under the Medal of Courage designation. Wrestling is not the only sport that he found a way to become a champion.

In college, he became a three-time boxing champion at the University of Tennessee and never lost a match. His flawless career led to his induction into the University of Tennessee Sigma Alpha Epsilon Boxing Hall of Fame. He loves these sports because no matter how good one looks in the gym while they are taking their mirror selfies, most people don't know how to respond when somebody punches them in the face. And even greater, how does one respond when life punches him in the face, and then drags him through the mud? Life punched Shay in the face repetitively as a child, and he learned how to respond with courage and determination. Some people will quit as soon as adversity strikes because they fear pain in any form. Greatness is made from resilience.

"I've always felt that someone is literally going to have to break my arm if they want to beat me."

Boxing and wrestling fine-tuned his mindset to become one of the greatest endurance athletes in the world.

Embrace the Suck and Become Ironman

The Ironman race is the most grueling race offered on the planet. It begins with a 2.4 mile (3.86 km) swim, followed by a 112 mile (180.25 km) bicycle ride, and then concludes with a marathon 26.22 mile (42.20 km) run. Some painful complications that are included, but not limited to any single one, are: cramping, heat exhaustion, urinating blood, fatigue, heat stroke, unbearable foot and back pain, plus much more. Shay deals easily with this misery, and, as he stated, *"I want to suffer."* He enjoys the challenge so much so that he has completed over sixty races, and he is ranked in the top one-percent class of performing Ironmen worldwide.

"I'm a believer that the Ironman Race chose me. My best finish was second, but I truly believe Ironman is a sport for me because it's not about who's the fastest - it's about who slows down the least. I really believe if someone is in a sporting event that's one hour or two hours, most people can do that. But, if they are asked to race a total of 140.6 miles in a lava field like I did in the World Championship in Kona, Hawaii, then it changes the playing field all together. A lot of things can go wrong. A lot of it is mental more than physical."

These athletes have to train their mind that they can and will finish every stroke, pedal, and step of the grueling 140.6 miles course. In order to cross the finish line, they must find a way to encourage their mind in every moment of the eight-hour-plus event. This is where his childhood experience became a strength for him, perhaps in a greater way than ever before. He is impervious to pain. He knows it is inevitable, and he chooses to embrace it.

"I start to urinate blood when I near the finish line. I'm very prone to dehydration because I can't sweat on one-third of my body. On the other two-thirds, I can't stop sweating, but I know I'm going to suffer every race, and so, when it comes, I welcome it. I know it's nothing new, whereas a lot of people when they start suffering, they start to panic.

"No matter what happens in the race, I will always cross the finish line. I've never not finished, and I've had some very challenging races. I had to run barefoot six miles in forty-two-degree weather in one of them. I had to push my bike before I was able to secure a tube to finish the biking portion. I've had an experience where I was peeing blood before I had to run a marathon through the Mojave Desert. So, I've encountered some situations that most normal people might say, 'Hey, today's not my day. Let's call it quits.'"

For Shay, it is all about crossing that finish line. No excuses. No distractions. The concept of quitting is foreign to him. Each person's potential greatest moment is defined when he or she finds the extra reserves in the fuel tank to push through adversity when most people would have given up. Accomplishing a worthwhile goal does not happen overnight in most instances. It can take decades, or an entire lifetime, to reach a goal, and it's what we learn during the process that shapes our character forevermore. He learned to "embrace the suck," because he knows that each moment of pain is an opportunity for character development. He learns something new about himself during each race.

"One of the things I've adopted over all my years in Ironman is called 'Embrace the suck'. What that means is that I know things will get really miserable, especially when I'm out there nine to ten hours in a race. I don't fight it. When it starts to happen, I embrace it. I call *to it and say, 'Hey I knew you were coming. I've got this'. This is when I shine. This is when most people would quit because times are getting tough, but I've prepared for this. I'm ready and I have nothing to worry about.'"*

The Cycle

Shay has found success in his family, in his Ironman events, and in his career, as well. He is the VP of strategic accounts for a healthcare firm just outside Nashville, Tennessee. His responsibilities include forming relationships with large hospital systems and gaining their commitment to partner with his company, so that his company can provide billing and collections services for these large hospital systems. He is made for this environment because it is a competitive, yet slow, sales cycle. Winning the business is often a reward from multiple years of hard work and persuasive selling, much like crossing the finish line of an Ironman race is the reward after ten hours of pushing through exhaustion. He views his business as a marathon, and he has never quit.

Not one single physician, friend, family member, church-goer, neighbor, or colleague would have imagined him finding elite success in athletics, in the corporate world, or with love and a family if they had been standing by his bedside when he was eight-years-old. He recognizes the cycle of life. There is a time to do push-ups in a pre-operating room because a surgery may strip someone of muscle functionality, and there is a time to wait in the midst of a long sales cycle with a large net-worth client, because impatience may lead to a premature mistake that can collapse the progress that has been made so far. There is a time to grieve late at night over a current condition of any sort (physical or emotional) with the constant reminder of the numerous scars present, and there is a time to leap for joy when crossing the finish line after the most tiring race on planet earth. Life is full of cycles, and he has chosen to embrace the miserable times and the surreal moments. Every step, every mishap, and every victory over adversity has made him the man he is today, and he would not change that for anything.

"Adversity has taught me to appreciate the gifts that I do have in life, and to never take anything for granted, because you can lose it just as quickly as you gained it, but equally as important, it's also to help others who are underdogs. I do what I can to help them obtain their goals, and the satisfaction I get from helping others often outweighs the satisfaction I get from helping myself."

Shay wants to help other underdogs who are in the midst of hardship. He is the author of <u>What the Fire Ignited: How Life's Worst Helped Me Achieve My Best</u> which is a deeper account of his story, and what he has learned during his life. He hopes that you, too, will embrace obstacles as opportunities that are only in disguise.

CHAPTER 3

Episode 3 - Radical Forgiveness

Chris Singleton

This Can't Be Real

I had just had a grueling study session in my Gainesville apartment. I was not prepared for the devastating news I was soon to hear.

I was just about to start my master's degree pursuit at the University of Florida the following week, in June 2015, and I was famished after studying all day for an entirely different education pursuit. The past few months had been filled with ten hour study days for the Medical College Admission Test also known as the MCAT. The only thing that freed me from more overworked brain cells was my evening jog that released the sweet adrenaline rush, so needed in the suffocating Florida heat.

When I returned home, I was hungrier than I was sweaty, so I decided to eat, then shower. Less than a minute into watching the news, I suddenly wasn't hungry, and my eyes were glued to the TV. My adrenaline spiked, and my arteries gaped open with my heart pounding like the energizer bunny.

The newscaster relayed the sad news: "Nine Dead in Church Shooting".

No other stress that I had been dealing with before mattered in that moment. "This can't be real." I thought. Then, I murmured it.

Then, I shouted it.

Nine black church members dead in Charleston, South Carolina, with one white supremacist suspect in custody.

Cynthia Marie Graham Hurd, Susie Jackson, Ethel Lee Lance, Depayne Middleton-Doctor, Clementa C. Pinckney, Tywanza Sanders, Daniel Simmons, Myra Thompson, and Sharonda Coleman-Singleton were the names on the victim list.

The story saturated every news channel in the market the following days and weeks. The rest of the week, I struggled to stay focused with my study schedule, but I witnessed something that I will remember forever, unlike any of the MCAT material that I had memorized back then. A young, eighteen-year-old man, was displayed on the world's stage, and he showed more strength and courage than I had ever seen in any man who was his senior.

Chris Singleton, the son of victim, Sharonda Coleman-Singleton, stepped up to the microphone and said, "We already forgive him [Dylan Roof] for what he's done, and there's nothing but love from our side of the family." This was less than twenty-four hours after her death. A town was still grieving. A community was still enraged. Families were still broken. Yet, in the midst of all of this commotion, stood a deafening sentence from a leading light in the community that would begin the path to healing for Charleston, and the entire world.

Black and White

"Adversity sees no color, it sees no change. It doesn't care how much money you have in the bank. It happens to everyone, and the adversity that I've gone through at such a young age has shaped me to be the man I am today."

Charleston, South Carolina is 67.4% white and 26.9% black according to the Charleston Regional Development Alliance. The citizens of Charleston were mourning the loss of nine loved ones, regardless if they themselves were black or white. Each person's reaction to that grief however was very different. Chris had to process his own grief while tending to his siblings and even to his community.

"I was used as a shoulder to cry on. When my little brother found out that night that our mother had been murdered, I slept in the bed with him, and he wept all night. I couldn't leave his side. At the time he was only eleven-years-old, so it was heart breaking times ten for him."

How does one find the words to comfort their siblings when they are searching for comfort themselves? He recognized his role as a consoling brother, and his new role as the leader of the family the very night of this horrific tragedy. At eighteen-years-old, he had to grow up much faster than anyone can imagine. He accepted his responsibility to support his brother and sister.

He did not make excuses.

He did not seek bloodshed revenge.

He picked up the shattered pieces of his heart and his siblings' hearts, and began the process of creating a new family identity. One that was still guided by Sharonda's love for her children, and his new step into manhood.

"I feel like I was chosen for that moment and for that time, not because of the bad things that happened, but because of the good that could come from it."

Racism often rips our communities apart and divides our nation. From my point of view, there is no excuse for racism or prejudice in either direction. No, it's not okay for great grandpa, who lives in rural Alabama, to mutter racial slurs at every Thanksgiving gathering just because that's "just how he grew up". It is time for the people of all generations to grow up and stand up to people who exhibit prejudice, even if the person doing it is an elder in their own families. The grandpa may call them out, and the mom might be embarrassed that they corrected him, but the person must overlook a few moments of familial awkwardness to make a lasting impact. Everyone should strive to be a difference-maker with integrity, rather than feel the paradoxical comfort of making it through another family gathering by muffling their voice.

Racist statements are no longer funny and harmless, or acceptable. Young people who hear inappropriate prejudicial statements can be led to believe the statements are, in some way, true.

The individual making the comments sounds ignorant and cruel, and the innocent bystander may feel offended, or they may begin to believe that sentiment themselves. Repeated exposure to ignorant ideas can lead to bad behavior. Dylan Roof was a recipient of those type of comments which warped his judgment of humanity.

We are all not exactly alike, and thank God for that. Our country is made up of different races and cultures, and we speak different languages; which gives all of us the opportunity to hear different opinions and views on life. Can you imagine how boring life would be if we all looked the same and thought the same way? More people should pick up a new pair of shoes and stand together with a different community, rather than picking up a gavel of judgment to condemn that community based on preconceived beliefs. We can all learn from each other, and we can all love one another, despite our skin colors, and despite our cultural differences. Step up to the plate, and stand for what is right.

Talk the Talk and Walk the Walk

"Hate cannot drive out hate. Only love can do that," were the famous words of Dr. Martin Luther King Jr. He stood for the wellbeing of all people, no matter the color, in a time when our country was in turmoil during the Civil Rights movement. Chris' passion and example exemplifies this American hero.

A few hours after the violence, he began to ask himself, "How am I going to tell my brother and sister?" Chris' father had been an alcoholic his entire life before he passed away in 2017, and Chris knew that he would not be able to reach him, because his father was probably drunk. He didn't know whom to call or how to share the news with his little brother and sister.

I'm sure Chris felt like he was drowning in grief, and suffocating from the inability to inhale with hope, and exhale with a plan of action. This eighteen-year-old did not know what the future held, but he knew that the first step he must take would be the most difficult and controversial. He responded in a manner that is similar to how his Savior, Jesus Christ, would respond to the Charleston Shootings.

"I didn't know what to say or what to do, but forgiveness was on my heart as soon as it happened. Why was it on my heart? I personally say it was the Lord. Some say it was the way I was raised. What he (Dylan) had done in that moment in time was already done. I wasn't going to get my mom back. What switched in my mind then was, 'How can I make things better now?'"

Forgiveness?! What about anger? What about paying Dylan back ten-fold for what he did to his mother and her friends? Dylan methodically planned and orchestrated a massacre because of his irrational belief in his own racial superiority. And, he did it at the most innocent and loving place that Chris grew up in - his home church. Only a few would have blamed Chris for having the wrong motive if he desired to seek revenge because almost everyone wanted to do the same.

"The thing with me is, that I believe that the anger wasn't going to get me anywhere. It was just going to be lingering over my head for the rest of my life. When it happened, there was sadness rather than anger. I didn't have a chance for anger to enter my mind or body, because I was so broken. I just wished I could spend more time with my mother. I never wished anything bad upon the person that killed my mother. My main thinking on that, is that it is very easy to let anger rule my thoughts, and rule out all the good things that can happen. Even to this day when I talk about someone murdering my mother, I try not to think about it as someone taking her life, but in a way that it was her time to go."

When I first heard him say this, I was speechless. His courage is admirable whether you agree with his stance or not. His response is how we should fight racism and live out Dr. King's famous words.

Dylan did not expect forgiveness from his victim's family. He expected a mutiny. He expected revenge to beget more racial violence, and for his actions to cascade to magnified results and areas throughout the country. He hoped that his plot would destroy Chris' hopes and dreams for the future. He hoped that Chris and members of the black community would just give up. He was certain that no good thing would be a result of his decision. Dylan Roof did not ruin Chris nor his perspective on love. He did not split the city of Charleston into racial war. Dylan lost.

Bouncing Back with Baseball

The most difficult step in recovery is beginning with the first. Chris is a baseball player, and he needed to return to the diamond to heal himself and his family. The world was watching, and he knew that his pursuit of his passion would stir up hope in others around him. Yet again, Chris proved his maturity before he laced up his cleats.

"After this happened, I reached out to my brother and sister and asked them, 'If you want me to stay with you guys, I will and I won't go back to playing baseball anymore, because I know that's going to be a lot of my time.' They both agreed that my dream was to be a professional baseball player and playing baseball was what Mama would want me to do. They gave me even more drive and even more fuel to my fire to work hard and train every single day, because I had a goal in mind."

So, he returned to a sport that predominantly consists of white athletes. His teammates and his school rallied around him. He knew his mother looked down from Heaven upon him every time he stepped up to the plate for Charleston Southern University. And the world watched. Would he struggle with the demographics surrounding him, given the events that just unfolded? Would he return violence with violence if the forgiveness in his heart withered away? Would his view of white people change?

In response, he said, *"Honestly, I haven't struggled with racism because of the way I was raised. In high school, before I met my fiancé, I had a white girlfriend and brought her home to meet my mom, and there were no questions. My mom just said, "Oh, you like this girl? Then cool." It takes a parent to teach their child to not hate another skin color, or think differently of another skin color. Some of my best friends are white, and there was no change in my heart. I always tell people who may have racial thoughts or say racist things, 'Dude, if there's anyone that deserves to hate another skin color, it is me because of what happened to my mom. But I don't, so that gives you no right to as well.'"*

Parents must teach their child how to respect and appreciate all skin colors. Sharonda instilled this in Chris from an early age, and this imprint is still evident in his life. She also instilled in him a hard work ethic that he made his own as he grew up. One that carried onto the baseball field. He went on to soar in his collegiate career as a centerfielder at Charleston Southern University. He caught the eye of professional scouts. In 2017, he was drafted by the Chicago Cubs in the nineteenth round, and he is still a part of their farm system today. He was drafted by one of the most prestigious teams in baseball history. He had achieved his dream.

"It was one of the happiest days of my life. As an athlete, I worked my whole life to become professional. I remember when I was eleven-years-old and I told my mom that I dreamed of playing professional baseball and she told me, 'Okay, well we got to work for it then.' She would write in the composition notebook the goals that I needed to set, and the schools I wanted to go to at such a young age. For me to finally get that call on draft day; it was like a joyful feeling that I can't even describe because I worked for something my whole life, and I finally heard my name called. It was amazing. I shed a tear and looked up to the sky because my mother and father were gone, and I knew that they both would be so proud of me."

Chris heard his name called on draft day, but it wasn't the first time he was called upon to do something remarkable. He is an underdog, but he used the power of God's love to direct him through life. He made it to the majors in a sport where so many try, and so many come up short. He was drafted by one of the nation's most beloved teams where the history of the franchise is just as vibrant as the ivy that covers the Wrigley Field walls. He provided for his little sister and his little brother in addition to providing for his fiancé and newborn son. He was the prime example of how to respond to racial violence. He accomplished all of this, and much more, while over-coming a national tragedy in his community, and losing his mother much too soon. He stepped up to the plate.

Sharonda Singleton's Memory

He thinks of his mother every day and wants to live life by faith as She did.

"She loved the Lord, and she was a kind person. She worked with people who had special needs, because she was a speech pathologist. She worked with people who couldn't communicate like ordinary people, and she was always smiling. She would read the Bible cover-to-cover every year. I don't know if there was a favorite Scripture that she had, but she liked a lot of Scriptures about adversity. There's one Scripture that I'm pretty fond of which is Proverbs 24:10, 'If a man falters in the day of trouble, he is a man of little strength.' I think this played close to my life and my mother's life, and what she dealt with from my father being an alcoholic. Whenever I saw it in her Bible, I knew it was something significant."

I believe that Sharonda would have responded in the exact same manner as Chris did after the shootings if she were still alive today, given his description of her. I know that she was highly regarded by all of her friends and peers and was a shining light on this earth that was taken away too soon. He is living out her legacy day-in and day-out.

He recognizes that he will carry this experience with him forever, and it is not something that he shies away from talking about. Dylan meant to strike evil against the city of Charleston with his decision, but Chris is going to use that violence for the good of society moving forward. Dylan meant to harm him with his evil actions, but Chris is going to use what was intended for evil and use it for good. Despite the evil Dylan perpetrated, Chris found a marvelous way for this tragedy to be used as his platform to speak up against racism and educate others with love.

"I realized awhile back that this is going to be part of my life forever. And rightfully so, it was a huge, traumatic event. I'm going to use it to better people's lives. I'm going to use it for the opposite way it was supposed to be used. Dylan's plan didn't happen at all; in fact, the exact opposite is happening. That's what I want to do with my life. I'm not going to stop in say, 2025, from talking about it. I'm going to talk about it the rest of my life, so that I can change maybe one person's mind that's thinking about doing the same thing."

And that is exactly how anyone can fight racism. Speak up against it in kindness and love, not animosity and revenge, in the hope that someone's perspective will be changed forever.

Chris travels the country during the offseason to spread his message of hope, love, and overcoming adversity. In January of 2018, he came to Austin to speak at the University of Texas. I had the opportunity to meet with him, his fiancé, and his newborn son after his speech and show them around Austin.

It was difficult to grasp the reality of our time spent together in that present moment, because I remember how nervous I was to reach out to him over social media when I requested an interview. Chris was the first person that I interviewed for the podcast that was outside my immediate circle of friends or peers. At the time, I did not have a referral from anyone else, or the credibility that I have today, to ask him for an interview. All I had was blind faith and a lasting impression from his statement of forgiveness that I remembered two years ago. I was overjoyed when he agreed to an interview, and it was a pleasure to show him and his family some of the wonderful spots in Austin. It was evident during our few hours together that he viewed life with endless joy. He has changed the world through his love for others, and it gains more traction every time he shares his story.

You can find out more information about Chris at www. thechrissingleton.com and you can follow him on Twitter and Instagram @csingleton_2.

"I speak on loving one another. Martin Luther King Jr. said, 'Hate can't drive out hate, only love can do that.' So, when I say love is stronger than hate, I really just want to trump hate with love. So if we love one another, that's the key."

CHAPTER 4

Episode 23 - One Leg Up on Life

Christy Wise

Paddleboard

Christy Wise made her way to Shalimar, Florida for leave from the Air Force base in Valdosta, Georgia. She flew an HC-130J plane in Afghanistan, the task of which is to refuel helicopters while in flight. Nothing sounded better than spending time with friends on the beach, so she considered this trip a perfect opportunity to refresh her mind and spirit before heading back to base.

Christy and her friends were stand-up paddle-boarding one late afternoon when life instantly changed from relaxation mode to survival mode. A speeding boat did not slow down as it quickly approached her on her board. She made a leap into the water in an attempt to save herself from an imminent impact. When she came up for air, after diving to avoid the boat, she saw blood everywhere in the water. Her severed right leg was only hanging on by the hamstring muscle.

Her fight for survival began.

Hanging onto Life

"I was stand-up paddle-boarding right behind my friend's house. That day, a boat swerved into the cove. It was just past sunset, and we were wearing huge headlamps. I took the headlamp off, and waved it at the boat. I fully expected them to go one way or the other. It took me a couple seconds to realize, 'Oh wow, they are not going to turn,' and that's when I jumped in the water to avoid it."

She attributes her fortunate decision making to her guardian angel because after she was hit in the shoulder by the boat, she immediately pushed off the boat and swam down. The force of her push off the boat was enough for most of her body to avoid the propeller except for her right leg. This all happened within a few seconds and she knows that there was not enough time for her to consciously think, process, and react to push off the boat and save her life. She considers it the first of many miracles that contributed to her survival.

When she surfaced, the seawater surrounding her began to mix with the color red. Her boyfriend at the time quickly helped her and used his t-shirt as a tourniquet. She recalls her body reacting without her mind making the conscious effort to react. At the rate she was losing blood, she was unable to swim to the nearest dock. Instead, the next miracle happened. She had tried to signal the boat that hit her with her headlamp before the impact. Somehow, the headlamp was still in her right hand when she surfaced after she got hit by the boat and the propeller. In the middle of the cove, with blood pouring out at a drastic rate, her instincts had enough wherewithal to shine the headlamp at a fishing boat to signal the people on board for help. That was miracle number two, and it also saved her life.

The boat that hit her never stopped, but luckily the couple in the fishing boat witnessed the entire accident and saw Christy's signal for help. They sped over to her as fast as they could. They finished tightening the tourniquet once she was in the fishing boat.

Though she felt she was out of immediate peril, her life was still in dire straits.

"It was a pretty crazy three minutes. I lost about 65-70% of my

blood in that amount of time because the propeller severed my femoral artery and went right through my knee. Another thirty seconds or so, and I wouldn't be sharing my story today."

She was fortunate to have survived. The United States Coast Guard's data for 2017 states there were 31 deaths as a result of 172 boating propeller accidents. There was a 15% fatality rate for boating accidents of all kinds in the United States.

Her military training played a large role in her survival because when she surfaced, she remained calm. Panic did not grip her. Her outcome may not have been the same without her training and sharpened survival skills.

"I was so calm. And the first thing I thought when I surfaced was, 'Dang, I should have had a brighter flashlight.'"

Christy knew that every passing minute decreased her chance of living. It's incredible how the body can shield the mind from panic when in shock. She was able to stay calm and focused in the water after the collision, and it was only when the first responders showed up on scene that she realized the severity of her injury. When the firefighters approached her, they did not have a sense of urgency that may come as you expect because she was so calm, too calm. The people surrounding her were more anxious than she was. However, the firefighters' were struck with the bitterness of plight when they removed the towel from her leg.

"My leg was still hanging on by the hamstring. The propeller had pretty much gone through the kneecap and everything else which is actually the worst-case scenario."

I'm a Pilot

The back of an ambulance can paint life in a picture that no other experience can. The hope of saving her leg was minimal, but her hope to keep her life was not. In fact, she was so confident that she would survive, that her moment of life flashing before her eyes left her with an imprint of a colleague's perseverance as well.

"In pilot training, in 2009-2011, there was a guy that I knew of that graduated one year ahead of me, and he got back to flying after an amputation. In the back of the ambulance, this was one of my first thoughts, 'Oh shoot the schedulers are going to be mad at me, and this is going to take me off the flying schedule for a while; but worst-case scenario, if Ryan did it, then I can do it.' So that's pretty cool that fifteen minutes later I was already thinking worst case scenario if I don't have this leg anymore, I know somebody that has done it."

Christy already had the mindset moments after her accident that her injury would not deter her from her passion for flying. Nothing was going to stand in her way.

The ambulance sped down the highway to the hospital, yet it was in a distant second place to the way the news of her injury spread throughout her network. Family and friends knelt in an instant to plead with God to spare her life. That prayer was answered.

She received tremendous support from the military community while she held onto her hope to return to the sky. Other amputee pilots reached out to her at the hospital to encourage her within days of her surgery.

"In the Air Force, everybody likes to say I'm the first female ampu-tee pilot and that I made history, which is definitely true, but I don't ever think of myself as a girl pilot. I think of myself as a pilot. So when people usually say that, I correct them and say, 'No, I wasn't the first pilot. I'm the sixth pilot. I'm the sixth Air Force pilot to return to flying after an amputation.'

Her refusal to accept her recognition as the first female pilot is one of the most incredible attributes that I find with Christy. Many people want to embrace the title of being the first or receiving first place. Yet, even though she made history, she wants others to view her simply as an Air Force pilot. She does not want others to think she is more special or more important than the other pilots. She is humble beyond measure.

Of the five other amputee pilots, two or three of them called her within days of her admittance to the hospital. She still doesn't know how they found out about her that quickly, or how they obtained her cell phone number, but she was overwhelmed with hope when she spoke with them. They all told her to call them for support and advice when she was ready to begin recovery and get back to flying.

It was just that simple. Nothing would deter her from returning to the sky. She had five other supportive heroes who had done so who were cheering for her from day one in recovery.

The doctors and nurses were in disbelief that she was even alive. They had seen many boating accidents and most of the time, their attempt to revive the patient was unsuccessful. One healthcare professional accidentally told her that everything would be all right because she would be able to retire, and the military would take care of her with overflowing benefits. This was said with the intent to comfort, but that didn't sit well with her. She was a pilot and a "dang good one." Those benefits were going to go to a retired veteran who needed it instead. She knew that she was more than capable to perform her duties and return to her squadron. This inspired her more when she began her physical therapy program.

"In the beginning of physical therapy, I was the strongest that I have ever been in my life. I had to wait for my amputation prosthetic line to heal before I received a prosthetic leg, and that took four to six weeks. So, there's a long time that I crutched around. All I did for eight hours a day when I got released from the hospital was work out. I crutched everywhere, I lost weight, and, all of a sudden, I started doing sets of seven pull-ups which I have never done in my life. So, I joked with my brother, 'this is what it's like to be a professional athlete!' because he's a professional skier. Before I lost my leg, I could only do four or five pull-ups in a row."

Although she was surrounded by her family, friends, and the support of many others throughout the nation, she still faced her own mental battle She dealt with the loss of her leg in a positive manner, choosing to see the opportunity to grow stronger.

The mental adversity that she faced was the most challenging during the middle of her recovery. Her incision line took longer than expected to heal, and there were issues with her prosthetic leg fitting correctly. She originally had a goal to return to her squadron within four months, but these delays made her miss her mark.

"Being patient was the hardest part. I knew I was going to get back eventually, but it took longer than what I wanted it to take."

Patience is often an adversary, rather than a companion. She is a highly driven individual, so her long recovery time struck her hard when she didn't meet her goals on time. She sometimes found herself wishing she could stand on two legs, rather than on one leg and one prosthetic leg. Past memories that constantly remind people of a better time in life are frustrations that everyone struggles with. Those memories can paralyze a person for days, or for an entire life if they only dream of that moment in time when they experienced harmonious peace. Sadly, peace often seems unattainable, and that can crush the soul's hope for the future. A person can be convinced that the past elated experiences will never be matched again. Comparison of the past versus the prospective future can be detrimental.

"The first time that anything became tough, I started wishing for my life with two legs again. I had this guy in rehab, who is a double below leg amputee from Iraq, who told me something that I had to write down, and I try to think about it all of the time. He said, 'Don't, for one second, long for what you were, but recklessly pursue what you can become'. That has become my life motto. The second I long for my life with two legs I realize that I can't do that. My leg is never coming back. I also like how he said it, not just pursue what you can become, but recklessly pursue what you can become. Through this, I can become stronger and better. Who am I going to become through it? These are the options that I have before me."

Her family is quick to remind her of this veteran's wise words whenever she faces adversity. That quote changed her life, and so did the support of another. In her corner stood a friend who calmed her frustration, reassured her of her inevitable glorious return, and made her laugh when she needed it most.

"I feel like the most blessed human being ever. I have a twin sister,

Jessica, who is a doctor. I always joke with people that I don't recommend losing a leg, but if you're going to lose one, you might as well have a twin sister who is a doctor!"

Jessica was finishing her last rotation for medical school in Las Vegas at the time of the accident. She jumped on the first flight to Florida once she heard the news. She spent the next few weeks supporting Christy by her hospital bedside. Eventually, Christy was transferred to the Center for the Intrepid, which is the military rehab center for amputees in San Antonio, Texas, and Jessica had to return to school in Las Vegas.

The Colonel of the hospital in San Antonio visited with Christy and asked her if there was anything that he could do for her. She immediately asked him if he could pull some strings to allow Jessica to finish her medical school rotation in San Antonio even though Jessica wasn't a member of the military.

It was a long shot for Jessica to be transferred to a military hospital especially near the end of her rotation, but the bond of sisters, especially twin sisters, is thicker than blood, and the military surprised them with an approval. Jessica moved to San Antonio and worked at the hospital where Christy was doing her rehab. This was the third miracle and may have been the most unexpected blessing of the entire process for Christy and one that surely helped her return to the cockpit.

Training was filled with a lot of adjustments for Christy. Each day she prepared herself mentally to accomplish the physical demands of her duty. She was completely ready to soar in her plane, except for one last task.

"I had been doing the simulators all along. I never felt like I left the airplane even though I wasn't flying it in the actual air. But, the week leading up to my first flight, I was still struggling with the parking brake because the parking brake on a C130 is miserable. It takes 150lbs of force and it has to be even force on both sides, the right foot and the left foot, in order for it to set."

The media were all scheduled to be there to capture on film the first Air Force female amputee pilot to return to the sky. She considered sharing with the media that she would not be able to fly on her scheduled day until she finally set the parking brake on Thursday - one day before her scheduled flight. And so, on that Friday, July 22, 2016, she had a determined attitude and she met the standards in order to return to flying. Her passion came to fruition. The sixth Air Force amputee pilot had returned to the sky. She was back in her element and her happy place.

The most memorable moment of that day came from a visitor. *"One of the ones that had been first in the Air Force to return to the sky as an amputee, who had helped me through my whole recovery with tips, was able to be at the first flight. He drove up from Florida to see it. He told me that the first day is going to be really exciting for the first two seconds, and then it's going to be back to work. And he was right. That was what it felt like."*

It took her one year after her accident to return to the air for the Air Force and restart the dream that she had never doubted she could do. As late as October of 2018, she was scheduled to deploy to Iraq, and she embraces the opportunity to return overseas. She is "itching" to go because she doesn't believe that simply returning to the Air Force is enough. She wants to prove her worthiness outside of a field test. She wants to prove her value in the cockpit.

I have no doubt that she will.

One Leg Up On Life

She has used her unfortunate circumstance to benefit others on an international scale. Many people fall into depression and live in the past when tragedy strikes. Others are refined in the fire of tragedy. She was one of those people. Tragedy does not have to bring one down, it can make that person wiser and stronger. Thus, the tragedy becomes a blessing to many. However, only a handful of them aspire to impact others on a global scale. She formed a non-profit organization that is helping amputees in Haiti get back on their feet.

The mission of the "One Leg Up On Life" Foundation is to glorify God and help children live life to the fullest by providing prosthetic limbs to amputees who cannot afford them. She received overwhelming support from her local community where her injury took place. Many families and businesses in the Shalimar area knew of her since the accident involved a hit-and-run. Many of these people were interviewed by the police, while the sheriff's department investigated and were shocked to discover that she had survived. Support flowed in from almost every house on every street in every neighborhood for her, and she was so overwhelmed by all of it, that she decided to launch her non-profit in the exact location where her tragedy took place. What would be the first event of this new ambitious organization? A paddleboard race, of course.

"It was a pretty big deal to say, 'This is what I was doing, this is the location that I lost my leg, but I'm not going to be scared of the water. I'm not going to let that affect me. I'm going to take this and do something good with it. A lot of people in the city knew of me, so when we put up "One Leg Up On Life Foundation" flyers, a lot of people came out just to meet me because they knew about "the girl." We had it in August 2015 which was just a couple of months later after the accident."

She didn't know anything about starting a non-profit or how she would raise money. All she knew was that she had a story, she had her life still, and she had a vision to help others who were struggling with the same issues that she was going through.

Having a twin sister who is a doctor is a fortunate thing. It turns out that one finds the pot of gold on the other side of the rainbow when one has a twin sister who shares the same vision for the non-profit, and already has connections in place to get the ball rolling. Jessica had been traveling to the Dominican Republic for the past ten years, and her interest in third world medicine grew with every visit.

Christy realized that the United States was inundated with organizations that help amputees already and recognized the gap in amputee care in Haiti. Jessica lived in Haiti for six months after she moved there in 2010 to provide care and restoration after the horrendous earthquake. Jessica knew of five children amputees that she helped back then, and knew that they had most likely outgrown their prosthetics from that time. God aligned Christy's vision, Jessica's prior experience, and their sisterly love for one another at the perfect time to deliver life-changing care to the poorest country in the Western Hemisphere.

"We provide prostheses to kids or adults that are not able to afford them. It's all amputees that we target, but besides just their prosthetic legs, we care about their full health. We always bring physical therapists with us and a full team of people. I don't want to just give them a leg. I want to make sure they can actually walk with it, their balance is okay, and they are not compensating with their other leg."

Christy looks beyond the gift that is a prosthetic and hopes to heal mental and emotional wounds as well. She knows first-hand the challenges and frustrations that come with relearning how to walk with a leg that she can't feel. She knows what it feels like to fall down over and over again. She tries to teach all of the patients that they can flourish in every area of their life regardless of the adversity they faced previously.

"The weeks in Haiti are brutally hard. Those weeks are stressful because so many things come up; it's hot, tools break, I'm tired, I'm standing all day and working with these patients in the lab, and sometimes, no matter what I tell them, they don't understand what I'm saying.

"I taught this one patient how to run, and then fast forward a year, and I was trying to teach a new patient how to run with a prosthetic leg which is really difficult to do. I tried everything that I could, and he didn't get it. Then, one of my first patients, Kevin, told the other Haitian in Creole what to do. The patient that I first taught was now teaching this new patient, and that was the best moment to me. I had a tear, and that right there was worth it.

"The pain that I deal with, the frustration, the overwhelming emails and all of the logistics that go into running a nonprofit, researching

501c-3s when I was in the hospital and I didn't know how to start an official IRS-sanctioned nonprofit, all of that stuff is worth it, if I think about that one moment."

She decided that her gift of life was worth it. She learned that her story still had plenty of purpose. She discovered that her injury could bring healing to others in third world countries. There is no doubt that Christy is a special person with a unique inner drive to accomplish the goals she has set forth.

I first reached out to Christy for an interview because I thought it would be so incredible to interview the first woman to return to the sky as an amputee Air Force pilot. I thought that she would embrace that title because she accomplished something that no woman had done before. I tried to put myself in her shoes, and I considered the joy it would bring me to become the first person in history to accomplish a feat. When I first asked her for an interview, I didn't know that she considers herself the sixth pilot to return to the Air Force as an amputee, and I didn't know that she was impacting the poorest communities in Haiti with One Leg Up On Life. Her story left me in awe, and I admire her genuine humility. She has received tremendous applause from the public, but she is quick to dish out credit to everyone else who has helped her get to where she is today.

"People tend to put me on a pedestal now, 'this amputee pilot who is back to skydiving and has her own nonprofit.' They put me in a box with a Superwoman label, and I try to bring their image of me back down to reality. I'm a normal twenty-eight-year old pilot, but this crazy accident just happened to me. I had a lot of support from friends and family, and we decided to form One Leg Up On Life. I get overwhelmed by all of it on a daily basis. I joke with people that I can get back to flying an aircraft, but after that I might be walking to my car and I trip because of my prosthetic foot, and that's what does me in. I start bawling. I try to bring it back to reality and say, 'Hey, I'm just like you, we all have struggles every day. Try to see the big picture and surround yourself with the people who are going to motivate you and inspire you and that's what helps you get through it.'"

No one knows what good can come out of disaster. The police never found the captain of the boat that hit her in the water after months and months of investigation, unfortunately. However, she chooses to focus on her happiness to be alive. She is the walking and talking evidence of a life that, after tragedy strikes, is filled with overflowing abundance and purpose.

You can find out more information about Christy and her organization at www.oneleguponlife.org.

CHAPTER 5

Episode 32 – Drug Addict Turned Entrepreneur

Kacey Gorringe

First Impression

I met Kacey Gorringe at a real estate investor meet-up group that is held monthly in Austin, Texas. While I have not spent nearly the amount of time in real estate investing pursuits, nor found anywhere near the measure of success of those efforts as Kacey and others have, I still find real estate fascinating, and recognize the tremendous return on investment of real estate acquisitions in an investment portfolio. During one particular "meet up," I met him, and we talked for a considerable amount of time, both before and after the meeting. We discussed the market, real estate goals, and other investors in the area.

Most "expert investors" can offer astounding strategies on how to make a large profit on fix-and-flips, buy-and-holds, or other forms of real estate investing. However, I find that most of those "big-wigs" are the exact opposite of the person that I want to become. In my opinion, a lot of them are prideful, pompous, conniving, and stuck-up. Kacey, on the other hand, offered tremendous advice, but displayed a genuine humble nature in the fullest form. I knew that somehow, someway his life story was much different than the other investors' stories in the group. His extraordinary kindness was nonexistent amongst the other investors. I knew that I had not only found a mentor to learn from, but that I had found a friend as well, and I hoped to learn more of his story as our friendship grew.

He was given the opportunity to share his investment strategies to success as well as his personal story to the group a few months later. He invited me to attend and really stressed to me that I shouldn't miss it. I was thrilled to support my friend in the midst of his peers, and I knew that he had something deeper to share with the group than just real estate strategies, but I couldn't imagine what the topic may be. I was eager to discover his journey and why he became the genuine person that he is today.

When I took my seat in the conference room among sixty other members the following week, he gave a stellar presentation and shared a lot of wisdom about real estate acquisitions with the group. However, the end of the presentation caught me way off guard because it contained something about him that I never expected before. He projected a picture of his old mug shot from jail on the giant screen at the front of the room.

Kacey was previously found guilty of drug possession. He was addicted to heroin for a long part of his life. All of the top real estate investors in Austin now knew what he had been involved with before becoming an entrepreneur.

None of us could believe what our eyes were beholding or what he was sharing. He was the most likeable guy in the group and seemed flawless, but everyone has a story and some of the details are more disgraceful than others.

Kacey has a dark past, but he decided to make a radical change that propelled him to become the positive influence that he is today. He concluded his presentation by defining why he chooses to do what he does as an entrepreneur and as a person, especially given his troubled history.

I knew that I had to interview him about his journey to a drug-free life because I witnessed many of my friends succumb to the powerful influence of drug usage. His underdog story began with a plethora of his own mistakes, but it was not the determination of his character, nor the final outcome of his life.

Curiosity

American citizens are currently in the midst of the largest opioid crisis in history. Opioids are substances that reduce the intensity of pain. In 2017, the United States Department of Health and Human Services (HHS) declared a public health emergency to combat the opioid crisis. More than sixty-percent of all drug overdose deaths involved an opioid, and since 1999, overdose deaths have increased by more than five times. More than 42,000 people per year die due to opioid overdose in the United States. The access to prescription drugs and illegal drugs is much easier than at any time in prior history.

Kacey grew up in Salt Lake City, Utah before he moved to Austin, Texas at twenty-eight years old. Family support for him overflowed in his household. His home environment wasn't the stereotypical environment a person may envision for a teenager to begin drug use. His home was one filled with love, security, and safety.

Many people wander why others try drugs. Are they uneducated? Are they trying to escape a current pain? Do they lack adult role models and subsequently have become rebellious? For Kacey, it began with curiosity.

"I think, just as most teenagers are, I was curious about trying alcohol and drugs, and unfortunately, I had a mentality of wanting to try as many things as I could get my hands on, and I think it ultimately stemmed from my insecurities. I never really felt like I fit in with a specific group, and, as everyone knows, middle school can be somewhat traumatizing to some extent. I found a group of what I considered friends at the time; obviously, they weren't, but they were people that accepted me, and we were curious about trying drugs. I started

smoking marijuana and drinking alcohol.

"I first experimented with drugs when I was fifteen-years-old, and by the time I was seventeen, I was doing ecstasy and cocaine. When I turned eighteen, I met someone that could get a prescription to oxycontin, and so, I started dealing drugs at eighteen-years-old. I was introduced to heroin when that oxycontin supply ran out. Heroin has about twice the potency of oxycontin, but about a fifth of the price. So unfortunately, a lot of people gravitate toward heroin. All of the horror stories you've heard about heroin are one hundred percent true. Heroin is the devil's drug. It's quite scary."

He was surrounded by a loving family. He was raised with good morals and proper values. He was in a good school district with a stellar education curriculum. He was taught from a young age that drugs were bad. He knew the harmful side effects before he began to explore this route with his friends. Yet, the lure of the curiosity of drugs tempted him more than the desire to logically refrain from drugs like his education taught him.

"I knew that drugs were bad, of course, and I knew that they led people down paths that usually didn't derive a positive outcome, but in the beginning, I was somewhat naïve, and I honestly didn't care. I was just doing it because it was fun. Then, the drug addiction got to a point where it became an uncontrollable tornado. I was trying to hold on to this F5 tornado, and I was already in the funnel. Once I realized that it had taken over my life, it was too late. It takes a very dramatic experience in one's life to stop. That's usually a rock-bottom scenario, and everyone's scenario is different. Mine was a culmination of a lot of different events. By the time I realized what was happening, I had lost control of the reins."

Why didn't he simply quit? He knew his life path was on a downward spiral, but it didn't make a difference to him. The general public, the people that are not using drugs, often look down upon addicts and say, "Just quit. Have a stronger mentality, and drop the needle. You are ruining your life." Yet, quitting drug usage is much easier said, than done. Addiction is a powerful, controlling, and seductive illusion that can leave a person feeling like a madman without the specific substance. Quitting drugs takes a tremendous amount of effort, endurance, support, and inner reflection to become effective, and that still may not be enough.

Every day began with the thought of his addiction. He neglected every other aspect of his life. Users often experience withdrawal symptoms which include, but are not limited to; the cold sweats, body convulsions, or feeling "pins and needles" in the legs. In the midst of these side effects, Kacey still chose to neglect his other responsibilities and blessings.

"I completely destroyed my life, but luckily, I was able to come out of it. Unfortunately, I've lost a lot of good friends along the way."

Rock Bottom

A wake-up call to change direction in life is often needed in different seasons of each person's life. However, people often ignore the subtle signs until a dramatic event thumps them up on the side of the head. A growing addiction leads to a shrinking amount of self-control. He tried to quit multiple times, but didn't have any real success until he went to rehab. Even after rehab though, the unexpected pain of loss was enough to bring him back to the temporary relief found in a needle.

"At the time, I felt like I was committed to rehab because my parents pushed it on me, and I conceded. My one requirement going into rehab was that I paid for it, and it took me years to pay back that money to my parents. I felt at that point, if I was willing to pay for it, I was committed, and I was clean for about three or four months during rehab. Then, a really close friend of mine overdosed and died from heroin. Unfortunately, I had not been sober long enough to be able to face those realities of a drug life and of what that brings, and so, that was a trigger for me, and I relapsed. I went into a deeper, darker hole at that point."

He has the utmost respect for rehab centers and the people that work there. Rehab centers are extremely beneficial and it was for him, but it wasn't the cure that he needed.

He was sliding down a slippery slope that he only gave a half-hearted effort to climb. Getting caught by the authorities was only a matter of time. Eventually, the punishment matched the crime, and it hit him heavily like nothing had ever done before.

"The final straw for me, when I got clean, was when I got arrested. I got caught with possession of heroin and cocaine, and I went to jail. I spent four days in jail, and for anyone that has ever withdrew off of opiates, they don't sleep typically, they shake uncontrollably, and sometimes they have the cold sweats. The worst part was when the police finally got in touch with my parents, and they came to visit me on day two or day three. I stared at them through a plate-glass window. I had a jumpsuit that said prisoner on it, and I asked them how my little brother was doing. I have a little brother who is now fourteen, and at the time he was about five or six. I completely broke down in tears, and of course when I was in the County Hilton as I call it, a.k.a. jail, I didn't want to show weakness. So, it was such a mix of emotions.

"That was my lowest point, and I had completely destroyed my life."

His time in jail was the turning point in his life, yet he had numerous and noticeable signs before his mug shot was taken. Stubbornness is a difficult characteristic to overcome. Here are some of the consequences that he suffered at the mercilessness of his addiction.

"I was over twenty-thousand dollars in debt, I dropped out of college, I lost my job, I lost an amazing girlfriend, and I pawned all of my personal belongings. I woke up every morning and picked up an acquaintance who I drove to a retail store, and he stole things to take them to the pawn shop and sell them for more drug money for us. I did thirty days of inpatient rehab, and I relapsed after that. I did so many drugs, specifically heroin and cocaine, that my small intestine collapsed, and I had major surgery on my small intestine. I still have a very noticeable scar above my belly button. I spent four days in the hospital, and the day I got out of the hospital, I used heroin again.

"I crashed my motorcycle, and broke my collarbone because I was so high on drugs. My parents changed the locks on their house because they no longer trusted me. I panhandled for money on the corner of streets. I went through hell and back."

Before his arrest, he worked in construction and purchased a house. Shortly after, he wasn't able to make his mortgage payment because all of the money that he made went to the purchase of more drugs. Right before he went to jail, he lost his house to foreclosure. It was 2009, and the economy was still recovering from the 2008 Recession, so the bank had trouble selling the property to a buyer because there wasn't much equity in the home. Kacey continued to live in the garage and sleep on a mattress on the ground before he was arrested for the possession of heroin and cocaine.

He had numerous reasons to admit his addiction's power over him, and declare his abstinence from substance abuse. The drugs were matches that he lit and played with, and they burned him every time. He only noticed the reality of how severely he was burned when he felt the cold metal of handcuffs lock around his wrists.

"I was at rock bottom when I finally got arrested, but that was such a blessing for me because that's when I finally realized I had three options: I'm either going to spend my time behind bars, I'm going to overdose and die, or I'm going to get clean. It really hit me when I was in jail looking at my parents through that plate-glass window."

The rock bottom of Kacey's life became the best disguised blessing of his life. The bang from the sliding cell door, and the distinct sound of the latch locking in place often lead to an inmate's evaluation of one's self. He was a criminal now. The curiosity of a teenager led to a felony as an adult. He failed society. He failed his parents. He failed himself.

Thankfully, he decided that although he had wandered down a path that most never turn back from, he could reverse course, and become the person he believed himself to be that lay deep down inside of him, even though it would come with abundant obstacles. Jail proved to be the significant and final halt that he needed to begin a true recovery. He began a true step toward recovery with his first step out from behind the bars.

The night that he got out of jail was a cold night in Salt Lake City. He wore a t-shirt and the shorts that he was arrested in a few days before. He had no money to his name so he borrowed someone's phone at a hotel. He call his mom who exhibited grace and took him back in for the millionth time. He was sick-and-tired of not recognizing the man that stood in front of the mirror because of his sunken eyes, dark eyelids, and his face that he picked to pieces as a result of doing meth and cocaine.

He knew that something had to change. He evaluated the substitute substance for opiate users, Suboxone when he was in rehab. This drug tricks the body to feel like it is receiving its dependence on opiates, but it is not detrimental to one's health. However, he knew that he needed to step out in faith and choose to not depend on any substance of any kind because he didn't believe in substituting one substance for another. He wanted to prove to himself that he could live without any drug of any kind. He went one hundred percent cold turkey without any form of a substance. For the first two weeks, he struggled to find sleep at all. At the six month mark, he completely stopped craving any type of drug and his life began to turn around.

When the dark cloak of heroin cravings were pulled back from his mind, his true character and integrity finally had a chance to shine through. Through all of the losses that he experienced, and all of the self-inflicted pain that he endured, he learned to utilize these experiences to benefit others moving forward.

Life is Calling

A new man with a new mission. He used resourcefulness, the ability to think quickly on his feet, persuasive skills, and delightful tact, but they were applied in the wrong context throughout most of his life. He knew that these natural attributes could be reformed, and he could trail blaze his life's purpose into moving forward. He just needed a chance. He needed someone to believe that his transformation was authentic. His mom saw the true yearning to change in her little boy's eyes. She was a professor at Westminster College in Salt Lake City and she found an opportunity for Kacey to go to college for free. He is eternally grateful for this opportunity, and it became his first opportunity to prove to everyone that he was a changed man. He graduated magna cum laude and was employed by a social media marketing company right after college finished.

"I was hired on as an account manager, but within six months, they realized that I was very personable, very outgoing, very charismatic, and that I was great with clients on the phone. So, they asked me if I would do cold calling for a given number of days, and they would pay me a hundred dollars for every meeting that I set up for our sales team. Within the first two weeks, I think I set up seven or eight meetings. Seven or eight hundred dollars was a lot of money to me at the time, so I started seeing dollar signs in sales. I found that I actually had a knack for sales, but I approached sales very differently than the old guard, if you will. I approached sales from a standpoint of empathy. I don't believe in the hard closing structure of sales. I think that sales process is flawed.

"Being good at sales, I quickly became one of the top sales reps for that company. I lasted there about three and a half years, and within those three and a half years, I really started to find myself, and find my calling, which is helping people and working with people."

A door of opportunity, to prove his genuine change, was opened. He walked right through it on his way to graduating with his degree. No one expected him to land the job that he did, and no one expected him to make the amount of money he was making legally after his conviction as a felon. The high life, but one that didn't involve drugs, was finally in his hands! Was it an incredible story of redemption, or did he just catch a lucky break that most people, especially most convicts, never experience?

His story could have ended with that last exclamation point. He established authority over his prior drug addiction. He earned his education. He ascended the career ladder within his company. This story would be well-deserving of applause if it ended there, but it did not, so the applause must wait until later. He craved something greater. His heart cried out within him for deeper fulfillment. He decided to enter the underdog arena again to change his life path, but this time, he did so as an aspiring entrepreneur. He quit his job to pursue dominion over his career and his life. Greed was not the cause for his career change. Ungratefulness did not play a role when he looked at his past and looked toward the future. Entitlement didn't exist in his resignation letter. Even with his troubled history, he knew that he could accomplish his dreams for the future.

Everyone, including his mother, thought that he was insane, because he was making over six figures per year. The owners of the company loved him, and he had the potential to move up the leadership ladder very quickly. However, Kacey knew that he wasn't happy and would never find fulfillment if he continued to build someone else's dream.

"I knew that I always had the entrepreneurial bug in me because my mother taught entrepreneurship and marketing at that college, and so I always wanted to do my own thing. I made the leap of faith when I knew that I was competent in sales, when I knew that I could go knock on doors, when I knew that I could cold call people, and when I knew that I had a way with people that was a little different than most salespeople. I made the leap of faith, and it was a tremendous risk."

Real estate investing became the apple of his eye. It was an entirely different industry with plenty of upside potential. The underdog spirit within him decided to trust his heart and work ethic, even though he had no prior experience in the market, and a foreclosure on his record.

"Before I closed my first real estate deal, I was two weeks away from being completely out of money, and not being able to pay my mortgage. It was quite the risk, but of course, with great risk potentially comes great reward, as well."

55

Turning Ambition into Reality

Kacey packed all of his belongings and moved to Austin, Texas to pursue his new desire. He hit the ground running immediately and tried to expand his real estate network within Austin at every opportunity.

His business was producing deals during its infancy, but now it is a well-oiled machine clicking on all cylinders, and creating hot leads frequently.

"My business is in real estate acquisitions. I have a fifty, fifty business partner and we specialize in a couple niches in real estate. One is foreclosure. We will either door knock, cold call, or send brochures to people that are in foreclosure. To go back to what I said earlier, I think the key to success in sales is expressing true empathy. When I reach out to these people, I simply say that the reason I'm reaching out is because I want to help them. I never lead with saying, "I want to buy your house," because if I'm truly not their best fit, and they can honestly and financially afford to keep their house, then I'm never going to tell them that they should sell me their house. That's just not how I operate. I'm a big believer in karma and doing the right thing. We have found that by approaching real estate, specifically with foreclosures in that way, we've been very successful because a lot of clients are realistic, and they realize that they are in over their head with their mortgage, and they trust us to help them navigate the sale. Sometimes, we'll purchase the property for ourselves, and do fix-and-flips as it is most popularly known, but sometimes we'll also bring in another investor, so we serve simply as a middleman, and then connect the end investor with a home owner as well."

Locking in the first deal took months and months for him. He believed that the only way for him to be successful in this pursuit was to dive-in head first. The life savings he earned in Utah and brought to Texas almost completely dried up like a shallow creek running through West Texas on a hot summer day. But his resilience found its stride, and he cashed in his first deal with two weeks of savings to spare. The time of barren opportunities are long gone for him now, because he produces a consistent amount of legitimate leads each week.

His positive fame in the Austin market grows with each deal, but he remains humble. He knows the work that had to be done to get his business to the point it is today, and he still believes that there is plenty of more work to be done to solidify his status as a trendsetter and a winner.

"I still have self-doubt every single day. The first five months of this business, I literally did not take a day off, because I couldn't afford to do so. I had a very small window, and I worked Saturdays and Sundays in addition to the weekdays. I think that I was so busy that I really couldn't even think about the doubt, but, of course, every day there is self-doubt. I mean I woke up this morning, and I just wasn't on my A-game. Everyone deals with that. Right?

"The moment that I did quit that job, and I no longer received those paychecks, it seemed like the world was against me. Everyone in Austin said the market was too saturated, and that I wouldn't be successful. I used that as fuel for the fire. I love when people tell me I can't do something now, because I don't have a big ego, and I'm not going to say, 'I told you so,' but I'm just going to prove it to them with massive success."

His profit margins per deal are often well above the average profit margin for other wholesalers. However, he does not let his numbers define him. He found his reasoning behind his motivation and his success. His moral compass always points to his true north.

Finding His Why

He is a firm believer that when a person discovers their "why" behind a goal, or their true purpose behind their goal to put it in another way, they will find appreciation in the pursuit, and much more fulfillment in the completion of the goal.

"Whenever we go through life, it's always going to be easier if we have a strong 'why.' It has been said, 'If your why is big enough, you'll

figure out any how to accomplish your dreams.' My why is multifaceted, but my biggest why is my little brother. He's fourteen now, and
I want to show him that the world is his oyster. He can truly change
the world. He doesn't need money to change the world. Yes, it helps,
but he can truly change the world by having a strong work ethic and
giving back to people."

Kacey is a huge believer in giving back. He wants to make the
largest positive impact possible during his life, and show others that
anything is possible.

"If I can come back from a ruthless drug addiction, being over
twenty thousand dollars in debt, losing my house, losing every personal belonging I have, after breaking everyone's trust, and if I can
spring back from that, and now be able to run a fairly successful real
estate business, then anyone can do this, anyone."

Kacey was a poor role model for his brother when he was a
drug addict. Honestly, that is the part that probably bothers him the
most from his past. He speaks all of the time about his little brother
whenever he meets new people. Even though his brother still lives
in Utah, Kacey's demeanor and his actions demonstrate integrity at
all times, as if his little brother was there watching him. Through the
redemption of a second chance, he realizes that he has been given a
great opportunity and a great responsibility to completely change his
brother's view of him. He will never fail in this area again, regardless
of what happens within or outside his business.

While he pours verbal affirmations and lessons about life into his
little brother, he also gives back to others throughout the Austin community. I have witnessed him giving hundreds of dollars to people
freely. He has given money to other investors for sharing strategies
with him in a ten minute conversation. I've seen him give money
to real estate club presidents as a sign of appreciation, since they
coordinate opportunities for him to network. The determination to
give is not because of bribery, instead, it comes from the genuine
nature of his heart. In fact, most people would never know that he
gives away so much money if the recipients of the money never made

announcements about his generosity, but they always do. The recipients are so blown away with gratitude that they want to publicly thank him.

Perhaps even more stunning than that is how he operates his business with clients after a deal is closed. He is quick to turn around and give a substantial portion of his profit back to the client. How many business owners do you know that donate some of their profits back to the customer that just gave the business owner their business? He does, and it's due to his "why."

The stressful process and time-consuming pain of foreclosure is all too familiar to him. He received no form of compensation when he was foreclosed on all of those years ago, and he remembers not having a place to live after the foreclosure process was over. He empathizes with his clients, because, although they are receiving payment for their house, the delinquent payments on their mortgage, which is the reason behind their acceptance of his help, are still pulling them down. He remembers when his next chapter of life seemed cold, dark, and unknown, with no place to go. He wants the extra money that he gives back to his clients to bless them with additional funds for living expenses, but even more so, he wants to bless them with peace and reassurance. The money he gives as a gift to his clients often leaves them in tears, because it is often the first sign of love and thoughtfulness that they have received in a very long time. That is his favorite part of the job.

His practice of giving back also spreads into areas outside of his work. He is no stranger to rolling up his sleeves and volunteering with community organizations throughout Austin and beyond. He does this because he knows that he can offer more than just financial assistance. He has been blessed with the ability to stand next to others and help them through their hardships.

At a business networking luncheon, Kacey expressed to others how he was eager to make a lot of money so that he could make the biggest impact. A gentleman asked him, "What's keeping you from making an impact right now?" The question hit Kacey deep within his heart. The profoundness of that question opened his eyes, and he understood that the most valuable asset in his life is his time, because he will never get it back. He can always make more money, but he cannot make more time. He immediately poured his servant's heart into the community.

"Once I realized that, it truly changed my perspective on life, and time is the most valuable to me now. I do a couple of things that I've been very consistent with; one is giving blood which really isn't giving time, but the ironic thing is that I am so scared of needles, yet I still give blood. I've been a consistent volunteer at the local Boys and Girls Club going on two years, and that is every Thursday afternoon for about two hours. That was a substantial time commitment when I tried to start my business. But when I started this business, I told myself there are two things that I refuse to sacrifice, one was my health, and the second was my volunteer work. When I volunteer at the local Boys and Girls Club, honestly, I think I get more out of it than the little first through fifth graders that I work with. I can have a horrible day at work and I leave to spend time with the little kids and help them with their homework, or play soccer with them, and suddenly, all of my worries go away.

"I don't really tell people this often, but anyone who's ever driven in my car, they'll see it. Whenever I go to the grocery store, I buy cans of fruit and give them away. I give the cans to anyone who begs on the street. I don't give them money because, again, I've been there, I know what it's like to panhandle, and I know what that money goes toward mostly, but instead, I give them fruit. I always have five or six cans of fruit in my car, and anytime I see a homeless person, I give one to them. It's not major. It's not making a huge impact, but it makes me feel good."

The same veins that were penetrated by needles filled with heroin are now penetrated with a needle to collect his blood and save another person's life. The great older brother that he wasn't able to be to his younger brother while he was in Utah is now a great role model to hundreds of "little brothers and sisters" at the Boys and Girls Club.

The same hands that once panhandled on the street for drug money is now giving nourishing food to those that are hungry. He has found multiple ways to use his past failures and experiences to help others avoid the same mistakes that he did.

He recently discovered a calling that is more profound than any other. We didn't talk about this during our interview because he had yet to devote himself to this new activity. But since the interview, he has volunteered a considerable amount of time in different states visiting prisons.

He has returned behind the prison walls, but, now, as a mentor, rather than an inmate. He frequently visits jails to share his past mistakes with the inmates and encourage them. He tells them that they, too, can make the effort to change their lives' courses and find a better calling, just like he did. He listens to them. He inspires them. He provides business training lessons to them. He loves those whom society has deemed them too dangerous to be loved.

He is not a failure, and he tells them that they aren't either if they choose to believe in the good in themselves.

Addicts lose sight of their purpose. They must be told that they are worthy enough to change their life despite their past mistakes. There is a reason why each person is here on this earth, but each person must find a better purpose on his or her own.

"The ironic thing is that a lot of people that I've met over the years that have been involved with ruthless addictions are some of the most intelligent people I know. I recently spoke to a rehab facility in Austin. It was about twelve men, and they were fresh off the streets, maybe two or three weeks clean. I told them my story, and I tell them, 'think of how resourceful you were at getting your fix. Now granted, you probably did some things that were illegal, but think of how resourceful you were. If you can apply that ingenuity, and that resourcefulness to doing something that makes an impact, Wow, think of how powerful that would be?'"

No Shame in No Regrets

I am thrilled that Kacey turned his life around and is the shining light in the Austin community that he is today. Yet, I've always wondered about Kacey and drug addicts at large. Do they ever feel unworthy to receive grace and live a redeeming life after all of the harm they caused themselves and others in the past? He is firm in his stance that anyone who fails can turn it around, and he changed my way of thinking about the topic forevermore.

"I don't consider myself unworthy to live the successful life that I am living now, given my past mistakes. I think about my past quite a bit, and, of course, I would reckon that almost anyone will say, 'if I would have known what I know now, if I would go back in time', but I honestly do not. I don't regret one thing. No, I don't think I'm unworthy, and I think everyone is worthy of building the life of their dreams. I study a lot of successful people and I would say the majority of successful people came from rough and tough beginnings. I think it just forges a stronger self-worth, and a stronger internal fortitude.

"I'm beyond grateful for what happened to me. I've always said this, 'if I can impact just one person's life to get them to avoid drug addiction, or to get them to make the leap of faith and start their own business, then that is a success in my eyes.'

"I am worthy of the life that I want, and so is everyone else. It ultimately boils down to how bad does that person want it?"

Yes, he wants to make a lot of money in his business. Yes, he wants to be financially free within the next couple of years. The pursuit of money, however, will not prevent him from striving to make a positive difference, and that is the worthiest cause that anyone can have.

"The other day, someone was speaking, and they said, 'don't just strive to make a dollar, strive to make a difference', and that's so true. I've always found it so ironic that there are people out there that want to build these empires at the expense of their community, at the expense of their personal and closest relationships, or at the expense of their health. I don't think wealth is measured by the number of zeroes

in my bank account. I think wealth is multifaceted: it's my personal relationships, it's my health, its success in general, and of course, everyone defines success differently, but for me success is defined as, how many people can I impact along the way? How can I not be lifted up myself, right? A rising tide lifts all the boats in the bay."

Kacey has become a great friend of mine and has impacted me in many areas of life. He inspires me in large ways, such as encouraging me to pursue my own business ventures with integrity along every step of the way. He inspires me in smaller ways, such as passing out cans of fruit to homeless people on street corners which has been something that I have done consistently since I interviewed him. And he inspires me to follow him on his mission to make a difference. For instance, we have plans to visit a prison together to encourage the inmates to become productive members of society. He is the most genuine man in Austin that I know. He is the prime example of a person with a troubled past who became a selfless underdog.

"Being an underdog makes me want my goals more. It fuels that fire, and again, I love when people tell me I can't do something, I love when people know my past and they think that I'm not going to make it because I was just a junkie. Bring it on baby, bring it on.

"I actually prefer to be an underdog because it's usually the underdogs that change the world."

CHAPTER 6

Episode 31 –
Gaining Weight to Empathize

Drew Manning

Wake Up Call

The alarm clock buzzes at 5:30 am and abruptly wakes you up from the best dream you've ever remembered on your cozy, California King, not so firm and not too soft, but perfect in the middle, bed. The dream involved delightful indulging of chocolate chip cookies, mint chocolate chip ice cream, and every flavor of glazed, sprinkled, frosted, and sugar-coated doughnut that you can imagine.

And now with the alarm clock ringing in your ear, that heavenly dream vanishes like an evil mirage. It's week three of your new health and fitness diet, and 5:30 am on Wednesday mornings is the time you agreed to go on a one-mile walk, a half-mile run, and ten minutes of calisthenics afterward. Doughnuts and sleep never seemed so enticing when contrasted to lacing up an old pair of sneakers to exercise.

Millions and millions of Americans desire to lose weight and feel fit. The mental, emotional, and physical benefits of fitness are common knowledge in today's society. The fountain of youth has yet to be discovered, but a healthy lifestyle is as close as one can get to increased longevity. Every New Year, people make it their top resolution to lose weight for their New Year and, sadly, many of those good intentions turn into excuses at about week two. Life gets too busy. The body aches from newfound muscles that the persons beginning their exercise regimen never knew they had, because they are so sore. Their desire for sleep reaches an all-time high level. Life becomes much easier to return to complacency and to the older routines of poor dieting and unhealthy lifestyle choices. Simply put, most Americans fail after a noble attempt is paired with feeble execution.

What about the opposite side? Most Americans would never dream of gaining unhealthy weight on purpose for their New Year's goal. Most already have unhealthy weight, so what would cause them to desire more?

Drew Manning was a modern-day Hercules. He was insanely physically fit, and was the guy that many people wished they could emulate.

Sometimes the adversity that a person faces is not random or unforeseen but is the result of the person placing the adversity on themselves with their own decision making. Drew didn't start off as an underdog but rather he chose to become an underdog to better understand the underdog mentality of his clients. He decided to gain as much weight as possible in six months and then lose it all in the following six months in a program he coined "Fit2Fat2Fit." By doing so, he completed his journey as an underdog because he persevered through moments of self-imposed discomfort and uncertainty. He stayed true to his clients to remain accountable to his plan, and he completely changed his outlook on himself, as well as others. He accomplished his twelve month goal of dramatic body transformation, and learned a lot about empathy during his journey to obesity and back.

First Love

Drew grew up in Salt Lake City, Utah with ten other brothers and sisters. He thrived with a competitive spirit because of his sibling circle and always wanted to be like his older brothers. His brothers played football and wrestled, so he wanted to do that, too. When he began playing in competitive school sports, his love for sports and physical activity grew with each tackle and takedown. His success in football and wrestling grew every year, and as he matured, he realized that the underlying theme behind his love for these activities was the ability to become fit and maintain fitness. His increased body fitness directly correlated with the amount of interest that people took in him.

"I got more attention from other people, and so, I noticed that other people's opinions started to matter to me. From an outside perspective, I was like, 'Oh, well if I'm fit and in shape, people will respect me more. They will be nice to me, and they will treat me well,' and that became part of my identity, and so over time, I judged my self-worth based on what my body looked like."

His career pursuit to become a personal trainer was the easiest decision he ever made, because it was a daily reassurance of his own ideal of his self-worth.

When identity is tied to something that is temporary, it often creates a recipe for inevitable heartache. Setting a fitness goal is something that everyone should strive to accomplish, but an identity should never be attached to a specific weight, muscle size, or a waist size, because minor fluctuations can crumble one's emotional side. Putting on a bravado outward appearance will only cover the hurt inside.

Drew became obsessed with fitness. He felt pudgy and worthless if he went two or three days without picking up a dumbbell. His own experience in the gym caused him to view fitness as a black-and-white reality; people either chose to be healthy or chose not to be healthy. There was no middle ground. Discipline in all areas of fitness was the only option for Drew, so he did not relate to the lifestyle choices of freedom from discipline that his clients often chose instead.

Drew needed a weight transformation on the outside to change his heart on the inside.

First Glance

Every waking moment for him was concerned with physical improvement and proper calorie intake. He placed unnecessary burdens and expectations on himself and on others. He was obsessed with his strict discipline, and found his client's lack of 100% self-control, inexcusable. To him, his obese clients were pitiful.

"I was more of a judgmental person back then, and a lot of people that are judgmental toward other people are usually a reflection of how they see themselves. So even though I looked great on the outside, I still hated who I was. I still thought I was never good enough, and that was the mentality, the culture, and the mindset that I grew up in. That carried over into becoming a personal trainer. I was judgmental toward other people. I thought that they could do better, and that they could be more disciplined, and instead, they were just being lazy. I couldn't figure out why it was so hard for people to just do what I told them to do. I gave them meal plans, I gave them workouts, and I became frustrated when they would gave me excuses like, 'Hey, you know Drew, this weekend was really stressful, and I went out, and I cheated on the meal plans even when you told me not to.' Or, 'I didn't get to the gym, because I was tired and sore.' I didn't understand why they did not just do what I told them to do. It was not that hard."

It's probably safe to say most personal trainers are driven by results, which is a good thing. The inability to place yourself in your client's shoes and express empathy, however, is a detrimental shortfall to them, and those in the industry, at large. He couldn't see the other side of things, because he never experienced a time in life when he was not in stellar shape.

Drew thought, *"You put down the junk food, you go to the gym, and, boom, you see results. It's easy for me. Why isn't it easy for you?"*

His clients told him, *'Drew you don't understand, because, for you, it's always been easy, and for us, it's hard."*

Reading books on obesity didn't work for him. Speaking with previously obese people who had become currently in shape didn't work. Reading the latest articles in magazines that shared new discoveries of exercise science didn't work either. His desire to gain a better understanding was present, but the method to get there was still in question.

When he first thought of gaining unhealthy weight on purpose, the idea sounded like a life calling to him. He knew that no other option would provide him with the knowledge and insight that he needed to understand.

After hearing the same story with the same excuses from his clients over and over again, he thought of a countercultural idea that would help him relate to his clients in a much better way. He decided to step into their shoes to literally become overweight. He decided to let himself go and gain as much weight as possible within six months without one exercise activity. The teacher decided to be humbled.

Gaining Weight on Purpose

Doughnuts, Coca-Cola, carrot cake, and potato chips were only a slim part of his daily food intake for six months. Nothing before ever seemed so sweet and freeing for him, at first.

"My rules for this whole journey were for six months, I couldn't do any exercise, and I could eat whatever I wanted to, but what I wanted to do was focus on everyday typical American food. I wanted to show people just how unhealthy these foods are, because sometimes we don't think they're that unhealthy for us, or sometimes these foods are marketed to us as health foods with labels such as fortified with vitamin A and vitamin D, or a good source of whole grains, or all-natural and low-fat. Those are the types of foods that I ate. A lot of highly processed foods that were cheap, affordable, and convenient, and I'll be honest with you, they tasted really good. I had a lot of sugary cereal like Cinnamon Toast Crunch, a lot sodas; of course, Mountain Dew is my beverage of choice, a lot of chips, cookies, crackers, white bread, white pasta, juices, granola bars, macaroni and cheese, hot pockets, and Spaghetti O's. You wouldn't believe how many hundreds of people emailed me during this journey and were like, 'Drew, you eat

exactly how I eat.'"

In the beginning, the joy of diet freedom was indescribable. His taste buds never had the opportunity in the past to enjoy mass quantities of delicious processed food that contained a high amount of fat and sugar content. The high of the transition came to a crash after four weeks. He began snoring at night which affected his sleep. His mood and his hormones were affected by his poor nutrition intake. Other side effects such as shortness of breath and an increased difficulty walking up stairs became a part of his life as well.

"I remember bending over to clip my toenails which was one of the hardest things I ever had to do, because I would have to bend over and hold my breath. I literally couldn't breathe because I had so much visceral fat around my organs. I would have to come up for air, and take breaks in between clipping my toenails which was crazy."

He went from being able to rep 225lbs ten times on a bench press without breaking a sweat to wiping beads of sweat off his nose after clipping ten toenails! The definition of embarrassment found a new meaning in him. While he grew larger, his perspective grew broader. He started to see things from the "other side" for the first time. His extra weight made him incapable to perform his past personal records in the weight room, yet he knew that would come. He didn't expect how the extra weight would drastically affect his mental and emotional capabilities.

"I knew I was going to get man boobs, and a big gut, and a big butt. I didn't realize how hard it was going to be, especially, on the mental and emotional side, which is where I learned the most valuable lessons."

Identity Crisis

Many Americans determine their self-worth by their net worth. A man thinks he is cool, because he has an expensive car. She thinks she is attractive, because she owns a big house. For others, they portray their self-worth on status within their peer group, whether that be as a college student, a boyfriend, a married man or woman, a lawyer, a business owner, a janitor, or a construction worker. The root cause for these misguided identities is possession. "What do I have, or what do I not have, compared to the person next to me?" I have a degree. She has a vacation planned to the Bahamas. He has six-pack abs. What happens when those material possessions or status bars slip away, or we just lose them suddenly? People often have a break down because they lose their possessions or status. Then their beliefs, egos, dreams, desires, confidence, and future plans depart, too.

It's difficult to separate the wheat from the chaff when trying to determine what is real versus what is fake in our social media driven culture today. Instagram, Snapchat, and Facebook are often used for presenting only the best side of each user, and many people hope that their followers will envy them, because they are living a fake highlife. The human race is constantly force-fed with marketing and advertisements from companies pitching their product, and promising the consumers how it will make the consumers feel better about themselves.

We are inundated with Hollywood and sports celebrities through various media telling us that happiness, love, and sexual desire comes to us only by having the perfect body. Social media is a constant reminder of this propaganda, and, sadly, many people buy into the lie. Our nation has an identity crisis bound up in possessions and status. It can only be fixed from the inside-out.

"Part of my identity was based on what my body looked like, and I think that goes for a lot of people who maybe experience the same thing. For my whole life, I was a fit, confident guy, but then once I lost that, I kind of freaked out. I didn't know who I was anymore without my body. I wanted to go up to complete strangers and tell them, 'I'm not really overweight. This really isn't me. Go to this web site. It's just an experiment.' I wanted to go tell people that, because I didn't have that confidence anymore and that self-esteem that I used to have."

Drew had to discover who he was without the six-pack abs. He needed to accept who he was when he looked at himself in the mirror and saw flab in his arms. He needed to find the most vulnerable and exposed part of his soul without the muscular physique surrounding him because that would lead him to discover his true identity.

"I remember an experience when my daughter was two. She was running around the house, and she wanted me to chase after her after I came home from work. I chased her for about a minute or two, and I was out of breath. I remember feeling super uncomfortable, super tired, super wiped out with no energy, and I sat down on the couch to take a break and she kept saying, 'No daddy! Come play!' I told her that, 'daddy is tired' and that 'I just can't'. She had these tears start to swell up in her eyes and started bawling, and she didn't understand why. She didn't know why I couldn't play with her, and she didn't know what I was doing to my body. In that moment, it really broke my heart because of the millions of people that can't play with their kids or their grandkids. Not so much because of their weight, but because of their health, and their energy levels. That's when I started to realize how much of this journey was becoming more mental and emotional than I ever imagined."

Drew was still a father, but in that moment, he didn't feel like a very valuable one. He felt worthless. He was out of shape and so far from his norm that he couldn't even play with his daughter after a long day at work. Every part of his identity as a super fit man that he had once used to describe himself had disappeared. He had to consider who he truly was in that moment when he was stripped from the powerful status he had once known and the only being left standing was the rawest version of himself. He had no rehearsal for this aspect of life.

His inability to play with his daughter for even a short period of time was more than enough reason to stop this experiment and return to a healthy lifestyle. The temptation to reverse course rang loudly in his thoughts, but he found the will to never give up and carry on in the journey, because he owed it to himself, and to others, to remain accountable to his plan.

The temptation to quit this experiment and return to his normal lifestyle remained ever present. However, he found the will to never give up because he wanted to remain accountable to his audience. A couple of months into his experiment, his story went viral, and he went on a media tour. His social media following grew significantly. He was still held accountable to his close family and friends who supported him during this life change, but he gained another responsibility because he had to remain accountable to a national audience, too.

Accountability partners are imperative to have when setting goals that are extremely outside of one's comfort zone. If a person aspires to lose fifty pounds in six months, and they have never lost that much weight, then they must find someone who can motivate them to continue toward progress when the days are tough. If someone wants to get out of massive credit card debt, then they should find a close friend who will monitor their spending habits, and how their money from work is being distributed appropriately across their expenses. An honest and caring accountability partner who can empathize with someone, but provide objective wisdom, will be a positive factor in the recipe for success.

He didn't want to let his growing national audience down, so he continued on the path to obesity. His body transformation was drastic, and is evidence of how a lack of exercise combined with a poor diet affects someone's physical, mental, and emotional health.

"I went from 193lbs to 269lbs, and from 8.5 percent body fat to 32 percent body fat. My waist went from 34 inches to 47.5 inches. My blood pressure was 167/113 at its highest. All of my lipids were in the red (harmful category)."

Six months completely changed his outlook on diet and life in general. His unhealthy weight gain was dangerous, and the side effects which included shortness of breath, interrupted sleep, and increased blood pressure were annoying burdens to carry. Still, with all of these statistical increases, he knew that this was part of the object of this journey, but his personality shift due to his hormone level changes was something that he did not expect.

"My testosterone also dropped to the low two-hundreds which

is something that people overlook when it comes to diet. They look at food as either this is going to make me gain weight, or this food is going to help me lose weight. We look at it like, 'How's this going to affect my physical appearance?' when in reality food affects us on so many more levels other than just our physical appearance. Once a person's hormones are affected by their diet and their lifestyle, then they become a different person, their personality shifts. A guy with low testosterone is not the same type of person that he was in his youth. The same thing goes for women with their estrogen, progesterone, and cortisol levels. Those were a few numbers of how quickly my body changed just over the course of six months."

After six months of lethargy, mood fluctuations, and wardrobe changes, it finally came time for Drew to begin the journey back to a healthy lifestyle.

Returning to a Healthy Lifestyle

One may imagine that Drew must have woke up on day one of the seventh month and tried to crank out as many push-ups as possible before jogging a few miles. However, he chose an alternative plan, and wanted to prove to his followers that a well-balanced diet is a crucial part of a healthy lifestyle. For the first thirty days on his journey back to health, he did not exercise at all, and only changed his diet. The results were amazing.

"I went from about five thousand calories of Cinnamon Toast Crunch and Mountain Dew, to two thousand calories [per day]. The first two weeks sucked. I remember that first day I had huge cravings. I felt starved all of the time. I felt moody. I felt grumpy and had headaches, and what I realized was that my body was going through withdrawal symptoms of missing those processed foods. In a way, I developed an addiction for it in just six months' time which was scary to me. I didn't realize this before how powerful that emotional connection to food really is, because I couldn't empathize with people before as a trainer. Before I said, 'Look, just put down the soda, and

stop eating the junk food. It's not that hard.' Then, here I was strug-
gling as a personal trainer that had only eaten this way for six months.
"Imagine someone that has eaten this way for their whole life.
Now, I was trying to tell myself, 'okay time to switch and eat real
whole food again', but my body fought back. It was like getting off of
a drug. My body didn't crave broccoli and spinach when I first gave it
those foods. It took a while to adjust to the real whole food. That was
a really powerful experience because it really opened up my eyes to
just how powerful the emotional connection to food really is for oth-
ers. That lasted for about two weeks. I remember feeling miserable,
even though I was eating spinach, kale shakes, vegetables, and all of
these healthy foods that I knew were going to make me feel good. I
didn't feel good, and I think people really related to that part of the
journey to see me humbled in a way."

He was so convinced of the effects of a proper diet that he
changed to a healthy well-balanced diet and still chose to refrain
from exercise for thirty days. In his opinion, Drew believes that the
discipline required with a consistent healthy diet is the most difficult
aspect of the journey to fitness for people. Drew lost nineteen pounds
that first month.

Proper nutrition for thirty days helped stabilize his hormone levels and make him feel better. He was more prepared physically to hit
the gym on day thirty-one than he was before, although he still had
to convince himself that he had the mental strength to do so. What
would people think of him when he returned to the gym and became
tired during an exercise way before he expected to? Would people
judge him for his physical appearance? Would other trainers mock
his effort? He worried what life would be like with a trainer's mind
trapped in an obese client's body.

"My testosterone more than doubled in that month, and all of my
blood work went back to normal levels within just thirty days of eating
clean. Eventually, I had to go back into the gym. I was still overweight.
I was nervous when I went back into the gym for the first time. I was
used to being the confident fit guy who wore cutoff sleeves shirts, and

here I was overweight, and I was wearing baggy clothes. I did not feel confident or sexy like I had before, and it was really embarrassing, because I was struggling to do push-ups with my knees touching the floor. I had lost so much strength, and it was truly devastating."

There is a beautiful metaphor that he discusses in his book, Fit2Fat2Fit, about this point in his journey. Before this life-changing journey, he envisioned himself as a personal trainer on top of a mountain, yelling to his clients at the bottom who were struggling to make the ascent. Words of encouragement and accountability flowed from his lips, but they fell on his clients' deaf ears, because it looks easy from the top of the mountain.

However, he switched positions with his clients on his first day back in the gym, and he was the one struggling to make the climb now. The view from the bottom of the mountain was completely different, and the ascent was much more difficult than he could have imagined.

He eventually lost all of the weight that he had purposefully gained, and all of his body statistics returned to their prior state in six months.

"I hit plateaus along the way, and there were weeks when I gained weight. There were weeks when I didn't lose any weight. I had all of the knowledge and discipline that a trainer has, and there were weeks when it didn't go perfectly, but there were a lot of valuable lessons I learned on this journey back to fit."

A Change in Perspective

One of the questions that I looked forward to asking Drew the most is, "Was it more difficult to gain the weight or to lose the weight?" I assume that most people would vote for losing the weight, because we have heard of those hardships many times from friends and family members who are trying to do so. However, most people haven't "let themselves go" on purpose to gain as much unhealthy weight as possible. In my opinion, the daily refusal to work out and create that endorphin release while already feeling lethargic, and force feeding myself with more Oreos to feel even lazier, would drive me insane. I believe readers can take away some wisdom from his response.

"A lot of people would assume that it was more difficult to lose the weight, but they were both different in certain aspects. It was hard to gain weight mentally, because I lost my identity. Mentally, it was really hard to be an overweight person for the first time in my life, and it taught me a lot about myself. Losing the weight was harder in a physical sense and emotional, because I missed that food. Physically, I started at the bottom of the mountain and it was mortifying. So they were both difficult in different ways, and a struggle in their own ways."

The light in which he viewed obesity will forever shine from another angle. Losing weight is not just about dropping pounds, it is about making a complete transformation of the person. A person needs to change his or her view of himself or herself in order to make a change in physique. Shedding pounds involves a complete mental, emotional, spiritual, and physical transformation. He learned that people truly don't care about how much you know until they know how much you care.

"My perspective is totally changed, and I realize just how wrong I was when it came to helping people and the way I was doing it. I was so focused on the physical side of transformation and helping people with meal plans, diets, calories, macros, exercise, workout programs, and their form. All of that is important, obviously, but that's not the key when it comes to transforming someone physically. People don't struggle with the knowledge. They're not lacking the knowledge of eating less and working out more. People struggle on the mental and emotional side.

"What changed me as a trainer was giving people the tools that they need to truly transform, which happens on the mental and emotional side. The real battle is won when I teach people how to love themselves along this journey, and help them with their own mental and emotional challenges. That's how a person makes it a true lifestyle change."

Today, he is comfortable in his own skin regardless of whether he is satisfied with his own physique or not, because he discovered his true identity that a mirror cannot determine when he stands in front of it. The environment in which he works provides an extensive amount of clients and other trainers who have never seen themselves as good enough, even though they may already have big muscles or a slim waist.

The only way to truly be comfortable with yourself is to love yourself and always strive to improve in all aspects of your life.

Drew knows many people who have six-pack abs but hate the person that they have become. The root of the problem is learning to love one's self. This journey helped Drew realize that, but he also met with a life coach who challenged him to view himself from a different perspective. Drew learned to meditate, and he embraced his own positive affirmations.

"If you can learn to love yourself the way you are now as you're working on a better version of yourself, then you'll be so much happier in the end. The time is now to learn to love yourself, because then all your relationships will change from how you love your spouse, your kids, and your friends."

Many people love to respond to others with "walk a mile in my shoes" when they face judgment or opposition. Drew had one of the most unique stories that I have ever heard, because he chose to walk in his clients' shoes for twelve months straight. Many in the public thought his idea for the Fit2Fat2Fit journey was outlandish and tomfoolery. He did not give up on his project. He remained accountable to himself and to his audience and to his peers and completed the impossible.

Drew is the author of the New York Times Best-Selling book Fit2Fat2Fit, which shares his emotional and mental experiences in the first half of the book, and his exact meal plan and workout regimen to get back to fit in the second half of the book. He is also the host of the TV show, "Fit2Fat2Fit", which follows personal trainers around the country who take on the same mission of unhealthy weight gain to eventually lose it in conjunction with their own clients who are struggling with weight loss.

He learned how to empathize, which is a skill that many people lack and overlook in today's society. He is a highly regarded trainer for many reasons, but his ability to empathize is the most telling. He underwent a complete transformation that started with denying himself his ego, shattered his old identity, developed a more honest one, and became a more fulfilled person because he learned how to love himself when his ideal self had been replaced with a less admirable one.

CHAPTER 7

Episode 30 – Fiercely Facing Abuse

Carolyn Colleen Bostrack

Single Mom

The responsibilities of a single mother are perhaps the most difficult responsibilities to uphold day-in and day-out. Cooking, cleaning, caring with love, and maintaining the requirements of a career are just some of the responsibilities that fall on one woman's shoulders with children. She is always expected to perform at the highest level in all areas of her life, because little tender lives depend on her.

Mothers are usually the gatekeeper for their children's experiences during their infant and toddler years. Crucial decisions are made during these early stages of life since the impact of the early years of childhood affects the child throughout their life, maybe even up to their last breath as an adult. Many mothers have the best intentions, but, sadly, they often use fear as an excuse to do what is convenient over what is the best for their child. The path of less resistance is chosen quite frequently. The fear of the loss of money, the fear of the loss of security, and the fear of the loss of protection are some of the factors that moms must consider when they make a decision to change their lifestyle for the sake of their children. One of the most fearful choices she can make is deciding whether or not to leave a man who supports her and her child financially, but abuses them physically, emotionally, and mentally.

Carolyn Colleen Bostrack lived through abuse day-in and day-out since her childhood. When she stepped into womanhood and had children of her own, she realized that the same cycle of abuse that she experienced as a child, and then as an adult, could likely become a living nightmare for her daughter as she got older.

She made the decision to be fierce by listening to her heart, leave her abuser behind, and face the challenges of the unknown, living in low income housing. This bold, but frightening, choice became the best decision that she ever made for herself, her daughter, and her future two sons.

A Child's Innocence

Carolyn had a childhood that no parent would wish for their own child. She grew accustomed to abuse during the early years of her life in Lacrosse, Wisconsin which left her with a distorted view of love.

Her innocence was stolen from her by her overly friendly neighbor at the age of four. The sexual abuse continued for the duration of time that she lived next door. She continued to experience mental, physical, and emotional abuse in other ways as well. Her mother was a hoarder and invited people who were down on their luck into their home. Her mother's intentions to help others were good, but the guests often had different intentions. Carolyn learned to hide her little sister in her mother's horde of things because some of the guests wanted to steal her little sister's innocence. Instead, Carolyn offered up herself in her sister's place to save her from those evil guests.

She grew up with unaddressed pain and did not have a role model to look to who demonstrated unconditional love. When she was sixteen, she almost overdosed on sleeping pills because she tried to numb the pain of a break up with her boyfriend after the break up combined with the normal stressors of a teenager, and mixed with the deep pain of her childhood. Thankfully, she woke up in the emergency room surrounded by healthcare providers who pumped her stomach free of the pills. She returned home to a little sister who was angry and hurt by what Carolyn had done.

"At that point in my life, I realized that my life was more than just my own, and that I had an obligation to my sister. I had an obligation to be a shining light to people that I may not have realized before. I promised my sister at that time that I would never quit on life again. I kept that promise to her, but that didn't mean that I didn't stop running from the pain. I ran into a relationship that reflected my self-worth. The relationship started off like most relationships, it was great, and it seemed wonderful. I learned very quickly that the relationship was not exactly what I thought it was, and I found myself in the middle of a very abusive relationship. I ended up pregnant, and I got married."

She had many guests enter her home as a child, but one can be lonely even surrounded by people. Most four year olds are fearless because they have nothing to fear when they play games outside with other friends or play with toys in the house. Yet, she lived in fear, because she couldn't trust anyone. The true definition of love was erased and replaced with manipulation. Her innocence disappeared. She was eleven-years-old when she became the protector of her three-year-old sister. She carried the responsibility of a parent to protect their child and sacrificed herself to do so. The horrors she experienced are unimaginable, and they are inexcusable of her perpetrators.

Coping mechanisms for abuse come in all different forms and severity levels. Many people choose to sweep pain "under the rug", and never want to discuss their emotions or memories. She learned to become expressionless and hold everything in. She decided to smile, to never cry, and to never show weakness. She pushed forward and tried to keep a positive attitude. In time, she realized that people do the most with the tools that they have, and she believes that is what happened with the people in her life. They had the tools to do what they knew how to do.

"I was running away from the emotion in the hurt, rather than processing through a lot of that hurt, and understanding that it wasn't my fault. I was running to a place in which to try and ease some of the pain that I was dealing with. That is how I ended up in my abusive relationship because that's all I knew. Comfort was within the uncertainty. Comfort was knowing how to navigate an abusive situation. That's how I ended up in the relationship that I was in because I understood abuse as love, and that was a comfort.

"Not until I decided to stop the cycle of abuse, did I realize what real love was, which is unconditional, compared to what real love isn't, which is unending self-sacrifice and suffering. Through borrowing the love that I had for my daughter, I was able to then stop, look, and realize what love could be and what it could truly mean. My journey to self-love began once I realized that true love is unconditional."

The journey to the realization of self-love was filled with pain and tough decisions. Motherhood requires gentleness and tenderness, but it also evokes fierce strength in certain situations. The "mother bear" mentality will come out when her "cub's" well-being is threatened. She showed no exception to this instinct.

Stepping Out in Fierce Faith

Determining one's life direction is often the result of one's faith or the lack thereof. Applying for a highly competitive dream job requires faith as well as action. Reestablishing trust in a person after a betrayal requires faith. Hoping that a relative will beat cancer requires faith. Leaving the person that is abusive requires faith, but it may require more faith than in any of the former examples, primarily in silencing the magnitude of fear. Her love for her daughter led her to take a giant step of faith to escape the abusive environment in which she lived. It was a step that she had never imagined taking, and she had to take it by herself.

"My husband would monitor my food intake so that I would stay

thin and remain attractive in his eyes. He would monitor my time in two-minute increments. He would monitor my money. He would monitor my phone conversations, because I was not allowed to speak to my friends or family. I really believed it was all because he loved me so much. He even went as far as saying that he loved me so much that if I were to ever leave, he would end my life and then his own, so that we could be together forever."

She was under the supervision of a manipulative monster. Their relationship was more similar to a dictatorship than it was a marriage. Her definition of love contained sexual abuse, mental abuse, physical abuse, and emotional abuse.

Her daughter became the sign at two-months-old that she needed to make a change and redefine what love meant in her mind. She needed to break the cycle of abuse and borrowed the love that she had for her daughter and make the necessary changes to move forward in life until her own self-love caught up to speed. She became the best mom that she knew how to be, and she knew that it required taking a daunting step of faith – she fled with her daughter from her husband.

"I escaped my abusive relationship. I found myself in the middle of a circle of poverty when I stood in line at the Salvation Army with nothing except for two boxes and a toddler bed. I just wondered where my next meal might come from. I was nervous. I was scared, and within that, I identified a way in which to map out a new definition of life for myself and my daughter, and to break free from the cycle of poverty by working sixty, or even seventy hours a week.

"I went to college full-time for several years until I was able to map out the next level and break out of that poverty and push on to something bigger and better. I stayed in the middle of a state of overwhelming anxiety; fear of the unknown and fear of my life being taken, as well. I was dealing with so many things that held me back, and that made me fearful, so I just wanted to hide."

Facing abject poverty alone is a terrifying task, and the fear is magnified when caring for a small child. Often, when women escape an abusive relationship, they are met with uncertainty in their financial situation, their ability to provide, their ability to protect themselves, and the risk of retaliation by their abuser. The National Domestic Violence Hotline states that, on average, a woman will leave an abusive relationship seven times before she leaves for good. She may return up to seven times, or even more times, due to a misguided love for the individual, in the hope that things will change for the better, due to the sense of normalcy of a life filled with abuse, the fear of physical violence from their abuser if they stay separated, and, sometimes, due to a lack of support and resources from the community.

Many victims lack a choice because their abusive partner provides housing, meals, medical insurance, and other benefits to them. Plus, abusive people are often manipulative, making it even more difficult for the victim to find the courage to leave. She found refuge at the Salvation Army. She didn't know where her next meal would come from or what the next day would bring, yet she found the courage to refuse the temptation to return to her abusive relationship.

"When I realized what love was supposed to be, my daughter was two months old, but that didn't mean that I left then. It was a struggle, and I didn't leave until she was thirteen months old. A whole year went by until I actually mustered up enough courage to take the leap of faith. It was the fear, and the fear of the unknown that kept me from leaving sooner. I knew how to navigate. I knew what to do to try and keep him happy, or keep him from being upset with me. I knew what to make for dinner, so that he would be a little bit happier, so that he wouldn't throw the food on the floor. I would think, 'okay, well, I'm just going to make it work. I'll make it work for just one more day.' The fear of not being worthy or deserving something more, the feeling of the unknown, and the fear of what would happen if I left with his threats, kept me in that relationship for that extra year."

Resources for women and children who were victims of domestic violence were available in the community, but Carolyn needed to take the time to learn about them. She often felt like she was alone even though she knew that resources existed.

When she finally left, it crossed her mind many times to return to that relationship. Skepticism of the future almost overcame the fear of her husband, but she stood her ground.

"Most definitely, there were times that life seemed more tolerable with him than at the Salvation Army. I didn't stay at the Salvation Army, because I was able to find low-income housing, but I needed a place to find meals, and the Salvation Army is where I went to get my meals. Yes, it was hard trying to figure out how to put food on the table, how to figure out how to make ends meet when I was also trying to go to school and be a mother. I definitely thought about returning to him because, again, I knew how to navigate an abusive relationship. It was like walking on eggshells. Eventually, he was going to have a blow-up, but I knew how to navigate the signs before the blow-up reaction so that it wouldn't happen as often. Still, it was a continuous battle of walking on eggshells around him, being afraid, and constantly under the thumb of another person."

She tried to deal with the pain of the past, the workload of the present, and her dreams for the future. Returning to him would only lead to additional abuse in the long run. She felt like she was juggling one hundred different parts of her life at once, and she knew that it was only a matter of time before her stressors caused her to burn out and crash. She did not want a crash to force her back into his household. This concern was recognized rather than ignored, and she developed a system to encourage herself to push through each to-do item five minutes at a time.

"I was determined to be the best mother that I could ever be. If I could accomplish anything in my life, out of all the failures that I saw within my short lifetime, if I could do anything, I would be the best parent that I could be. If I would have died tomorrow, then I know that my daughter would know that I had done everything within my power to give her a better life than my own. That meant that I needed to be the best person that I could be, and going back would [not allow me to do that]."

To become the best version of herself, Carolyn could not allow her daughter to grow up in a household of abuse. She realized that children often copy the path that a parent lays out for them. She shuddered when she thought of her daughter becoming a woman and dating someone like her father. The cycle of abuse would continue and she would have failed as a mother.

Pushing forward seemed like a monstrous effort. There were moments when the long-term future overwhelmed her with burden and she wasn't sure if she could persevere. What got her through each difficulty was finding the courage to push through each day five minutes at a time. The five minutes at a time mindset helped her build up to her goals by getting her through one day, one week, six months, and then, onto a year. She used that method through her undergrad college studies, through her master's degree, and onto her PhD while building her career and a life by design for her daughter.

By pushing through each moment of uncertainty five minutes at a time, she grew fierce in her determination and confidence. She became a single mother that was unstoppable in chasing her goals. She fiercely broke the cycle of abuse that she had known her entire life.

PhD in Motherhood

Carolyn has gone on to accomplish every goal that she has set for herself. This mother received her PhD in Organizational Leadership and Development, published her first book in 2016 and is working on her second book now, excels in her career, travels all over the world giving speaking engagements, and she does this all while being the best mom to her three awesome kids. Her goals become more challenging and more rewarding as time goes on. How does she make time for her career and education goals while being present for her children?

"It's all about intention."

She practices her "Miracle Morning" which is a method to success developed by Hal Elrod, each morning (Hal Elrod is a keynote speaker and best-selling author). She organizes each day with intention, and each day she practices her "Miracle Morning" with her children. They practice their affirmations together, they exercise together, they journal together, and they all strive to be the best human beings that they can be. This routine fulfills her soul and provides her with a lot of energy for the day.

She is deliberate when she coordinates her busy schedule, and she is intentional in her efforts to push back against hurtful memories of the past. The things that she has experienced do not magically go away. Her previous method for coping was to hold every single emotion and thought inside of her. She didn't open up to let anyone see the deepest parts of her heart. Now, she is learning to become more vulnerable because that's where her healing lies.

She went through many years of counseling to learn how to cope better. She recommends counseling to all victims of abuse, but she understands the difficult work that goes into a deep dive reflection of oneself. She is fond of the saying, "You can overestimate what you might be able to accomplish in one year, and underestimate what you might be able to accomplish in ten." She likes to consider herself a "ten year overnight success" because she will have flashbacks of her abuse that cause setbacks. However, she can identify the roadblocks faster than before and can process through them much more efficiently.

"I have learned to look back with a mindset of gratitude because no matter what happens to me, even if it's not my fault, I get to choose every day how I look at that, and how that mindset affects me. Looking back over the many years of abuse that wasn't my fault, I also look back from a state of gratitude, because I wouldn't be the person that I am today had I not learned those lessons. I wouldn't have the toolbox that I have today in which to cope toward the future because life doesn't always get easier, we just learn to cope a little bit better."

Living Life Fiercely Five Minutes at a Time

Take life in five-minute segments and, suddenly, the problems that you face don't seem as intimidating. F.I.E.R.C.E. stands for: Focused breath, Identify one goal, Examine and alternate barriers, Reflect on current perceptions, Co-create your own reality, and courage to Engage. Life becomes more manageable when these principles are applied. Success becomes attainable in five-minute daily dosages.

Her book is F.I.E.R.C.E. - Transforming Your Life in the Face of Adversity Five Minutes at a Time, and she still uses the methodology shared within. She has witnessed many people use this methodology who are fighting cancer, trying to lose weight, or setting goals for their business. She uses her book to pay it forward. She donates all of the proceeds to organizations that share similar values as her. One example is Gunderson Health System which is a mental health and social services fund that help people who are trying to get out of their current situation and help themselves. She loves to donate to the organizations who want to help the people who seek more out of their life.

Her goal setting never ceases. She is on a quest to better herself every day, and she hopes that many people she talks to will jump on board with her.

"I have many goals, but my life design and family goal is to be able to share the ability to design a life of their making for my kids, and teach that to millions of people. I've already had the opportunity and feel so grateful that I've been able to share this message with thousands of people. I want to take it to a higher level, and spread that word, but where I start is at home base. I make sure that my children are surrounded by like-minded people who realize that they can create a life by design."

She often reflects upon the days when she was rocking her two-month-old daughter to sleep and praying to God, "Please send me a sign. Please help. I'm not quite sure what to do." And she often thinks about the moment when she redefined what love meant to her. She smiles when she remembers these days of uncertainty and compares it to the day that she sent her daughter off to her first day of college. Tears were rolling down her face as her daughter exited her hug and walked away, but she knew that in her heart she had accomplished something she never would have experienced if she didn't break the cycle of abuse. Her daughter doesn't have to worry about the abuse of her father or the abuse of another male close to their family. Carolyn made it as a successful mother.

"The joy in my heart is to know that I did it. I am able to gift that joy to my kids, and just give them a life of minimal worries. I want to give them the opportunity to realize that life can be whatever they design it to be. I want to teach more people, parents, and communities that they should give back, because what they give is what they will receive, and life can be whatever they design."

Life by Design

If you are reading this, and you have been a victim of abuse, then Carolyn has some advice for you, specifically. She believes that life can become what you make of it. She knows the pain that you feel because she experienced it, too. She empathizes with you. She wants to see you choose to attack life fiercely with your dreams and ambitions. The time in your life is never too late to make a change and step out in faith.

"I would tell teenage girls that are currently facing abuse, 'don't stop dreaming'. If you ask any five-year-old, they can tell you immediately what they want to be and what they believe in. But, as we grow, and we go through middle school and high school, there are so many different things within the world that are barraging us and telling us that we can't do this, and we can't do that. I would say don't stop dreaming. Try to remember what it was that you absolutely adored and loved when you were younger. What if you could do anything that your heart desired? What if you woke up tomorrow and there were no barriers? What would that look like? So, keep dreaming about what you're passionate about. Continue to contribute. Keep realizing that you can create a life of your dreams. I would say that being an underdog has given me the tenacity and the determination to create a life of my design."

I encourage you to strive to become whatever you want to be. Don't let anyone try to stop you on the path to achieving your dreams through manipulation, bullying, or any form of abuse.

You can find out more about Carolyn at www.carolyncolleen. com. You can also buy her book, *F.I.E.R.C.E. - Transforming Your Life in the Face of Adversity Five Minutes at a Time,* on Amazon.

CHAPTER 8

Episode 38 – Cure Blindness
Dr. Geoff Tabin

Changing the World on a Grand Scale

"When we started what we are doing in Nepal, people said it was impossible. When we started the ascent of the East face of Mount Everest, people said it was impossible. When I have a few other like-minded people, a brotherhood or sisterhood forms of people who are like-minded, and who are willing to try what other people say is impossible. There is strength in numbers from being underdogs together. I think rather than being an underdog fighting alone, when you bond with other passionate underdogs, things work better."

A lot of children grow up believing that they will change the world on a grand scale, but only a few actually do so in adulthood. Steve Jobs, Bill Gates, and Henry Ford are some names that will live on throughout time due to their creativity, their vision, their inventions, their philanthropy, and their impact on the course of humanity.

Another name that you may or may not have heard of already is Dr. Geoff Tabin. He is not producing mass quantities of products that the average consumer uses every day; rather, he is increasing the life expectancy of patients in the developing world by two to three times with a ten-minute surgery. Over 600,000 people throughout the world have benefited from this surgery already.

The International Agency for the Prevention of Blindness states that approximately 217 million people throughout the world have moderate or severe distance vision impairment, and thirty-six million people are blind. Of those people who suffer from partial or complete blindness, 75% of those cases are avoidable.

In the developing world, many of the cases of blindness derive from untreated cataracts. This is a common procedure in the Western World of easily accessible healthcare, but it usually doesn't exist in the rural areas of developing countries where hospitals and clinics are rare to find. Untreated cataracts lead to complete blindness which can drop the life expectancy of an individual to one-third that of the average person who is not blind in that country due to their inability to make a living, search for food, and protect themselves.

Dr. Tabin was deeply saddened by the low quality of life these patients experienced during his travels abroad, specifically, in the Himalayan Region. The more people he interacted with that could not see due to cataracts, the more he knew what his life's calling would be. He continues to change the world because he restores vision to people who have been blind for decades. He gives them the gift of seeing their loved ones once more. He provides them with a longer, and a more colorful life.

At first glance, a white male doctor may seem like the exact opposite example of a compelling underdog story. After all, he afforded his education and is making more than enough money to be categorized in the upper class of our society. He is capable of living a luxurious dream life that is free from hardship. However, he prefers to submerse himself in the poorest areas of the world. The odds favor the side of failure when someone embarks on a mission to change the world. And, the probability of failure increases exponentially when one is trying to change the world while residing in another country, handling the responsibilities of a non-profit organization, treating patients in a medical practice setting, teaching medical students, creating sustainable solutions to world-wide public health issues, mountaineering the world's tallest mountains, and tending to his family. He is an underdog because of the magnitude of the goals that he has set off to accomplish. He challenged these improbable odds, succeeded in all areas, and truly changed the world.

Choosing Medicine

Dr. Tabin is a professor of Ophthalmology and Global Health at Stanford University. He teaches students about the diseases of the eye and how to treat them, all the while looking at bio-design and reverse engineering to bring top quality healthcare to the poorest countries in the world for a lower price. Treating patients and teaching students are two of his top three passions now, but it was the third passion of his, climbing, that brought him to the career he has today.

His grandparents were survivors of the Holocaust. They taught him that it is a privilege just to be alive, and that if someone is alive, then that person should be doing something to give back and make the world a better place. His grandmother believed that there was nothing more noble that a person could do than practice medicine, and that stuck in the back of his mind as he grew up.

He attended Yale University as an undergrad where he played collegiate tennis and fell in love with rock climbing. He finished his pre-med courses, but was unsure if medicine was the best career for him moving forward. Since he was not sure about applying to medical school, Yale nominated him for the Marshall Scholarship at Oxford University. He won the scholarship and studied moral philosophy. He explored the moral imperative of what every individual on the planet should have relative to basic rights, and he began to think about healthcare once again. Global medicine intrigued him more and more because he wanted to bring quality care to the poorest of the poor throughout the world.

During his time at Oxford, he was afforded the opportunity to travel to other continents to climb different mountain peaks. He was awarded the A.C. Irvine Grant in honor of Andy Irvine who died up high on the slopes of Mount Everest in 1924. This award paid him to go on climbing expeditions around the world, free of charge. His mountaineering experience increased and he became a tested climber.

After Oxford, he made the commitment to a medical profession-al pursuit, and he matriculated at Harvard Medical School. While at Harvard in 1983, he was invited to join the expedition team that was attempting to make the first ascent of the East face of Mount Everest which is the most difficult side of Everest to climb. He was offered this opportunity due to the climbing experience he gained at Oxford.

When he applied for his leave of absence to climb Mount Everest, he was met with opposition by a faculty member. The professor said that a young man in Harvard Medical School didn't stand a chance of receiving a leave of absence to go climb. Instead, he advised Dr. Tabin to apply to do research during his travel, because Harvard would give him a course credit for his trip. The professor happened to be an ophthalmologist interested in the effects of high altitude on retinal physiology, and he wanted Dr. Tabin to help him collect data while he was in the Himalayan Mountain Range. Dr. Tabin accepted his offer.

He made the trip and became a member of the first and only climbing expedition to successfully climb the East face of Mount Everest. During the ascent, he took pictures of his crew's eyes to study the effects of high altitude on the retina. This gave him a glimpse into the field of ophthalmology.

When he finished medical school, he began working as a general doctor in Nepal because he wanted to get involved with global medi-cine. However the big public health issues, such as: finding alterna-tive sources for clean water, providing better nutrition, and building an infrastructure for better sanitation were issues that an individual doctor couldn't impact by himself. He was just about to return to the United States when he witnessed the miracle of sight restoration. He saw that blindness was a burden on the community in more ways than one.

"It is a huge burden on a subsistence agrarian economy to have a blind person. Once a person is blind in the developing world, the life expectancy is less than a third of similar "age and health matched" peers. Blindness takes another person, often a child, out of the workforce or school, to care for the blind person. I saw a Dutch team come into the village that I was stationed in and perform cataract surgery with lens implants, and it was crazy! People just blossomed back to life with a joy that was so infectious. I thought this healing was the most amazing thing ever."

He returned to the United States, and for the first time in his life he knew exactly what he wanted to do for his career. Since he had done research on the eye during his ascent of Mount Everest, he was accepted into a great ophthalmology training program at Brown University, and then finished his fellowship in Australia. Finally, after all of his schooling was done, he returned to Nepal to work with his current partner, Dr. Sanduk Ruit. They began to reverse engineer the question, "How do we bring the same top quality of care that we give in the West to the poorest of the poor, at a cost that is affordable?" That question became their challenge, and the question is what they have tried to address with solutions for the past thirty years.

Climb Higher

There is no doubt in anyone's mind that Dr. Tabin is an incredible doctor. He is also a famous climber, not just because he climbed the East face of Mount Everest, which he did with his team in 1983, and no one has ever repeated the climb, but because he became the fourth person ever to reach the summit of the tallest peak on all seven continents. Climbing the tallest mountains in the world is extremely dangerous, and many people lost their lives trying to do so. A large unfavorable probability of success comes with this amazing and rare accomplishment. Yet, the seven summits were not a goal that he initially set out to accomplish.

Before his time at Oxford, he climbed Denali in Alaska the highest peak in North America. Then, while he was at Oxford, he climbed the North Face of Carstensz Pyramid, the highest mountain in Australasia, before he later joined the team that climbed Mount Everest.

After medical school, while he was searching for a way to get involved with global medicine, he was asked by a commercial trip company to lead an expedition up Vinson Massif, the tallest mountain in Antarctica. Despite the frigid weather and the lack of familiarity with his group before the trip, he successfully led them up and down the mountain.

On his way back down Vinson Massif, a person in the group hired him to guide him and his friends up Aconcagua, the tallest mountain in South America. After Dr. Tabin did that, he was left with only two more to go, Mount Elbrus in Europe, and Mount Kilimanjaro in Africa.

He crossed Mount Kilimanjaro off of his list after he finished his work as a general doctor in a refugee camp in the Democratic Republic of the Congo. In his last year of residency at Brown, he finished the seven summits with the easiest mountain to climb of the seven by climbing Mount Elbrus.

This daring, mountaineering doctor doesn't fit the mold of most physicians in hospitals. He believes that he can accomplish great progress in global healthcare while accomplishing his personal endeavors, even if they happen to be endeavors that he doesn't set out to do initially. Reaching the seven summits proved his resilience and determination. The development of those two traits prepared him to act on his passion to cure the world from blindness, one cataract surgery at a time.

Cataracts

Many people in America have cataract surgery, but many others have no idea how cataracts are detrimental to vision and the quality of life. He explains cataracts and how they can destroy vision when left untreated.

"The eye is like a camera. There are two angles, the front window

which is the cornea, and then the crystalline lens that focuses light onto the retina which is like the film of the camera. Then, the optic nerve brings the image to the brain which processes the image and informs the person what they see. As someone gets older, the lens of the eye slowly changes its color and gets little deposits. There are no blood vessels going through the lens of the eye to take away waste. The lens slowly gets cloudier and cloudier as time goes on.

"Most people in the West start losing their vision in their seventies or eighties. Our surgery is so good, that we just do it right away, but in the developing world, the cataracts come on a little bit sooner in life. The reasons are partially related to intense UV light and the lack of antioxidants in one's diet. The light causes oxidative damage, and when there are no antioxidants in a person's diet, the changes become more profound. Also, smoking or living in a smoke-filled hut, makes a big difference.

"The lens sits behind the pretty colored part of the eye called the iris, and it's kind of like a peanut M&M; the lens has an outer candy shell, although the texture of that shell is more like the skin of a grape, and then you have a little chocolate mess called the cortex, and then a hard peanut. As people get older, those inner parts in particular get very cloudy. In cataract surgeries, I open up that outer candy shell to take out all of the cloudy bits, and then in order to get very good vision, we measure the curvature of the eye, in order to put a lens implant back into the eye that will give very good focus, and perfect vision."

"Half of the blindness on our planet is from treatable cataracts which can be completely reversed."

The Himalayan Cataract Project

Dr. Ruit and Dr. Tabin are convinced that they can eradicate unnecessary blindness throughout the world. Yes, a large part of that is due to their surgery expertise, and they have restored vision to thousands by the work of their hands. However, they realize that in most medical mission trips, the medical care for the community that doctors provide concludes when those doctors return home. The restricted and short duration of access to healthcare is the limiting factor in global healthcare for the poorest communities. Both of these doctors strive for sustainability when they leave the country behind. They have created viable manufacturing processes, implementation plans, and education systems to support these communities. In addition, they have developed groundbreaking economic models to make sure these plans are self-sufficient financially.

"The person who is really the genius behind what we're doing is my partner in Nepal, Dr. Sanduk Ruit. He came from a small hill village with no running water, no electricity, and no schools, and he ended up graduating from the best medical school and training program in India. Then, he did a fellowship in the Netherlands, and then another in Australia."

When Dr. Tabin witnessed the Dutch team provide the life-altering cataract surgeries, he began to investigate what other medical professionals were doing in Nepal to address this issue. He discovered that there was no one in Nepal performing modern cataract surgery with a lens implant. The backlog of people who were totally blind and needed surgery was over 250,000 people.

"The World Health Organization declares someone being blind as someone who can't do the tasks of daily living. In America, we give legal benefits when a person can't see two lines down the eye chart. Well, the blind people in Nepal can only see the motion of a hand. They can't even count my fingers two inches in front of their face. They are totally dependent on others, and I saw that there was no one in the country doing modern eye surgery. I thought to myself, 'wow, this is a place that I could make a difference.'

Dr. Ruit created a system in which no one with more skills does anything that anyone with lesser skills can do. He trained doctors in Nepal to perform cataract surgery, and he reverse-engineered how to take the absolute best Western care, and deliver it at a cost that's affordable to the people of Nepal. By the time Dr. Tabin finished his combined four years of training at Brown University and in Australia, Dr. Ruit had been working for four years to address the issues surrounding the common method of third world healthcare. Dr. Ruit wanted to change the old standard of Western surgeons visiting third world countries, performing a few hundred surgeries, and then leaving, because he saw that access to healthcare became absent for the community as soon as that doctor left.

The motive and the blueprint was there, however, as in most circumstances, the greatest obstacle can be a shortage of funds to support a project. A cataract surgery cost over $200 before Dr. Ruit and Dr. Tabin put new processes into place. That cost to the patient was astronomical and simply unfeasible. They discovered a way to drop the price to $5, which is a 97% or greater reduction, through a self-sustaining economic model.

A cataract surgery at Stanford costs approximately $4,000, but Dr. Ruit and his team built the first manufacturing factory in Nepal which provided the means to produce a lens implant for $5 through locally sourced materials. By manufacturing in Nepal and India, they were able to bring the same quality instrumentation and the same quality lens implant, down to a very low price.

The next question that they needed to find a solution to was, "How do we do the surgery?" In the United States, the equipment that is used during a cataract surgery costs hundreds of thousands of dollars. These instruments were unfeasible in Nepal, so they decided to brainstorm tools that they could create to help the Nepalese people.

They found and adopted an incision technique that was published by an Israelian ophthalmologist. This technique required more skill, but it provided a means to forego the expensive equipment that was used in the Western world. Dr. Ruit and Dr. Tabin perfected this technique and began sharing it with others.

Dr. Tabin and Dr. Ruit started a world-class ophthalmology residency program in Nepal. At the time, Dr. Tabin was also teaching at the University of Utah, and he matched the curriculum at the University of Utah with the residency training program in Nepal. They also started training more nurses and ophthalmic technicians. They created a three-year program for ophthalmic technicians after high school. When they graduate, they can give glasses, screen a patient, and work in primary eye care centers in rural areas of the country where a doctor may not reside. Dr. Tabin and Dr. Ruit have created sustainable manufacturing plants and teaching programs to continue to heal the Nepal region of unnecessary blindness even when they are not operating on the patients themselves. They are helping the poorest of the poor both directly and indirectly.

"The other big thing that we did in Nepal was create a system which is called compassionate capitalism. The elite of the country, who previously would have gone out of the country to have their very expensive surgery, are now having their surgery in the country, and by engaging the powerful, we're able to reach the powerless, and provide for the powerless.

"And so, we are able to subsidize all of the care. In Kathmandu, there are probably forty percent of the patients that will pay several hundred dollars for an upgraded cataract surgery, which is exactly the same quality as what I'm doing here at Stanford for $4,000. We're making about a $600 profit on that procedure. We are able to charge about $100 for the surgeries that cost $25, and about thirty or forty percent of those patients are paying. Those paying patients, fully subsidize the free care for the poorest patients."

The cataract surgeries are done in high volume. Whenever Dr. Tabin finishes surgery on one patient in Nepal, he wipes his gloves down with absolute alcohol and moves to the next table where other healthcare professionals have already draped and prepared the patient to be ready for surgery. His team of surgeons can do as many as ten surgeries per hour per surgeon. The high volume provides the means to pay his doctors, nurses, and technicians well which further increases passion and well-being amongst the team.

"We're performing overall eye care training. The rate of blindness dropped from 0.88% back when we started in 1994, to 0.34% in 2012, and now, it's at about 0.23% (in 2018)."

They reverse-engineered a manufacturing process to provide locally sourced lens implants to patients of the same country. They dropped the cost of surgery by 97%. They created teaching programs to train local Nepalese people that continue caring for the sick when Dr. Tabin and Dr. Ruit are not around. They created a sustainable economic model to provide healthcare at a modest cost to the affluent in society, and at no cost to the poorest of the poor. They perfected an incision technique that allows them to finish a surgery in ten minutes and completely reverse a person's blindness and quality of life. They did all of this in a country that is devastated by poverty and blindness. And they are just getting started.

Expanding Across the Himalayan Region and into Africa

Dr. Tabin and Dr. Ruit have seen tremendous success in the Himalayan region. In fact, they have seen so much success, that they are now treating all forms of blindness, and not just cataracts. They never predicted that they would have grown at the rate they have so far.

"We called it the Himalayan Cataract Project because when we started in Nepal in 1994, there were only two doctors who were doing modern cataract surgery with lens implants. There was a backlog of 250,000 blind people. Only 15,000 surgeries were performed by Nepali surgeons a year. No one was doing modern cataract surgery in Sikkim, in Bhutan, all of northern India, West Bengal, no one in northern Pakistan, and no one in Tibet. So, we called it the Himalayan Cataract Project because we thought it would be a lifetime just to get a handle on the cataracts there. Now, Nepali surgeons are doing over 300,000 cataract surgeries a year. The quality is phenomenal. If I had to have my own personal cataract surgery, there are about ten surgeons I'd be happy to go to in Nepal to have it done."

They have expanded into Bhutan and have already developed a mature and sustainable system. The number one cause of poor vision is a lack of glasses, and they have a wonderful program that tries to reach every child that needs glasses in Nepal. They have trained retinal surgeons who are performing world-class retinal work in oculoplastics, neuro-ophthalmology, and corneal transplant surgery. The Himalayan Cataract Project is not simply a cataract program any longer, they are an overall blindness program, and the organization is reaching the most unreachable places.

"I take great pride in seeing some of our young protégé. In Nepal, we have several young superstars who are the next generation behind Dr. Ruit, and here in America, I have several unbelievable people who have done fellowships with me. We are also focusing their career on global ophthalmology, and we're starting to see a little bit of the same traction. There is the same development in Africa as well."

Now, the Himalayan Cataract Project is crossing the Indian Ocean. The two doctors have moved their organizational efforts into a new continent to establish their self-sustaining methods in African countries. They have begun a training program in Africa to replicate the same success they have found in the Himalayan region.

"We're also working in Africa. Our main programs are in Ghana, Ethiopia, and Rwanda, but we're doing quite a bit in several other African countries, too. I still get a kick out of post-operation day one, when people go from being totally blind to seeing. There's just no other miracle like that in medicine. We still have sixteen million people on the planet who are blind from cataracts, but the cool thing about doing the eye surgery, is once we operate on a person, they're no longer a statistic because they're cured one hundred percent."

What started as a regional project that seemed like a lifelong effort to attain at the beginning has turned into a global transformation of countless lives. They are experiencing the growth in miracles right now. Dr. Tabin and Dr. Ruit have, quite literally, changed the world.

One Step at a Time

Creating and coordinating a global organization, while setting up clinics in rural areas of Nepal, while teaching medical school classes at Stanford, while practicing medicine, while creating self-sufficient economic models of healthcare across the world, while caring for patients, and while climbing the tallest mountains on planet Earth may seem a bit overwhelming to most people. How does Dr. Tabin structure his days appropriately so that he can accomplish the tasks in front of him without feeling overburdened and stressed? The answer is by focusing on one task at a time.

"I think I would go crazy if I started to think about what I can't do, and all the things I have to do. The exact total emails in all of my inboxes that I have today are 20,817 unopened emails. I've got a fairly good ability to focus on what I'm doing right now, and basically block out the rest of the world. I try to focus on what I'm doing at the time, and I try to avoid thinking about what else I need to do. I do have a little mental list of what I have to get done in the immediate future, such as returning patient calls, and other important things for the people closest to me, but a lot of the other stuff, I just don't worry about.

"I love the twelve-hour operating days in Ethiopia when my mind is completely free, and all I'm focusing on, is just the eye that I'm operating on, or when I'm on a big rock climb for ten hours. I really love working in the developing world where my whole focus is purely on, 'how can I take the best care of this patient right now?'"

The organization's influence is spreading and providing sight restoration to millions of people from different cultures. This organization has no limits. They are preparing to make an impact in every corner of the globe.

Changing the World on a Continuous Scale

"My personal short-term goal is to make the same progress in quality in Ghana, Ethiopia and Rwanda, that we have made in Bhutan, Nepal and Sikkim. I'd love to create momentum that really overcomes

needless blindness throughout the world. It's such a travesty, because for the amount of money that the American government spends every month on our wars in Iraq and Afghanistan currently, we could restore sight to every needlessly blind person on the planet. We would have a whole lot more friends, and have a whole lot less animosity in the world if we did that."

He hopes to witness a few African countries that have completely adopted his methods of manufacturing, teaching, and implementing by the time that he retires. He continues to drive awareness by sharing studies that have shown the cost recovery to the economy in one year for sight restoration provides four dollars back to the local economy for every one dollar spent on sight restoration. He hopes that many governments and philanthropies can view blindness as a major problem and work in a collaborative effort to end blindness throughout the world.

The Himalayan Cataract Project began with two men who dreamed that they could make a difference in the most remote areas of the world, but they figured it would take their entire lives to see their goals come to fruition in Nepal. In twenty-five years, their vision has transcended small villages in Nepal to reach the entire Himalayan Region and the jungles of Africa. I believe it is fitting that they began in the region of the world with the tallest mountains because their vision to change the world started much like Dr. Tabin's first step to ascend Mount Everest. They are much closer to the completion of their ascent to cure the world from blindness than when they started in 1994.

Dr. Tabin found the will to never give up when he climbed the tallest mountain on all seven continents. That same will to succeed will not cease until every person receives the gift of a prolonged life that comes with the blessing of restored sight. Steve Jobs said, "The people who are crazy enough to think they can change the world, are the ones who do." Dr. Tabin and Dr. Ruit are filled with abundant passion to silence their critics, and erase blindness from civilization. They are the crazy ones that we are eternally grateful for.

Dr. Tabin is the author of <u>Blind Corners: Adventures on Seven Continents</u> which are stories of his climbing adventures. In addition, the Himalayan Cataract Project's story, and the two men behind the organization, are written about in <u>Second Suns: Two Trailblazing Doctors and Their Quest to Cure Blindness, One Pair of Eyes at a Time</u> by David Oliver Relin. You can research more information about this incredible organization at <u>www.cureblindness.org</u>.

Episode 13 – Twenty-five Years in Prison for a Crime He Did Not Commit

Michael Morton

Yellow Tape

"I often joke about the fact that I used to be a statistical midpoint in the American demographic. My wife and I were incredibly average. I had a routine every morning and left for work like I always did ..."

Michael Morton was living well in the middle-class lifestyle in the booming city of Austin, Texas. Each morning was a replica of the previous day's pattern. He would fire up his engine to head to his management position at a local grocery store. Routine. The Morton's lives seemed to him to be predictable as the rising of the sun and just as exhilarating as watching the grass grow. Routine. There was nothing out of the ordinary that had happened to him or his wife, Christine, or Chris, for short, throughout their entire relationship, and for all intents and purposes, there seemed to be an unwavering trajectory of an uninterrupted life to normalcy ahead of them. Routine. Then, on August 13, 1986, they were catapulted into a bizarre future.

Michael left his job at the usual time to pick up his three-year-old son, Eric, from the babysitter. However, he was only met with a perplexed expression from the babysitter when she opened the door to find him standing there. Worry began to churn in his stomach. Eric wasn't there, and Chris had never dropped him off that day. He knew Chris would have called him at work if she had adjusted their routine. She was always precise and never forgot to share important details with him, especially the whereabouts of their son. He quickly called home. On the other end of the line, he heard a deep southern drawl coming from the county sheriff.

"Michael, we need you to come home now."

Michael immediately punched the gas pedal to the floorboard.

"Shortly after my departure to work a man came in the back of my house and murdered my wife. He beat her to death in our bed. The police did not contact me right away after they found her body. It wasn't until I called home that the sheriff picked up the phone, and told me to come home immediately. When I got to my home, it was like one of those movie scenes where the house is surrounded by police cars and there is a big yellow crime scene tape around the house. The sheriff, right there in the front yard, told me my wife was dead. Nothing prepares you for that."

His average life was gone forever.

Crumbling

What would you do if you were stranded on an island by yourself? How would you survive? I would bet that most of you have played that game with friends or in an education setting with a teacher at some point in childhood. Our hypothesized reactions to sudden changes in plots can consume our conversation with friends, and hijack our individual day-dreaming. But most people find it difficult to imagine how they would react to the murder of a spouse.

"The more catastrophic the event, the less likely you are to accurately predict how you will behave. What I was going through when I got that news is absolute stunned perception. It was like I was falling.

My hands and my feet were tingling, and now, I know, this is the textbook fight or flight reaction. I felt like I was breaking into a million pieces and I was falling inwardly. On the outside I was told I looked like I was very stoic, but my responses were internal, they were not outward."

Michael's wife, his best friend, was beaten to death in the same bed that they had made love in countless times. His son had lost his mother. The wound was like no other.

Plus he soon discovered he was the main suspect in the case. This came a few days after the crime in the midst of trying to process these new emotions of the death of his wife. He lost his wife, and a rising tide of rumors and speculation by the sheriff's office began to persuade everyone in the community that he was the culprit. Friends and family started to turn away before he could make eye contact with them. Suddenly, no one answered his calls. At work, he sensed people were whispering behind his back. Chris' killer was still on the loose.

"About six weeks after my wife's murder a lot of stuff had happened. I hired attorneys because it was clear that I was the suspect. It didn't appear an arrest was imminent. The police were having problems from my perspective.

"I was in the kitchen one evening with my son, and we were preparing dinner. There was a knock at the door, so I picked up my son, and when I answered the front door, it was the sheriff and deputies, and the sheriff announced he was there to arrest me. I was completely stunned. I didn't see it coming. And as bad as being arrested was, the worst part was when they pulled my son out of my arms, because he did not want to leave me."

Michael had just lost his wife, the height of tragedy. He lost his son now, too. He felt emasculated and stripped of his identity as he rode out feeling like he had been tar-and-feathered in the back of a police car for the entire community to see.

"There was nothing that I could do. I had no choice. I tried to put myself in my son's shoes, and the only thing I could think of was the

last time my son had seen the police, they were in our house and it was a really bad day. And now, they were back and he was terrified. They gave my son to a neighbor. They handcuffed me and marched me to the front of the house, and put me in the backseat of a police car. I never saw the world from that perspective or myself from that perspective before. It changed me as well because it was a very concrete example and tangible experience of the power of the state. The power was that they were going to put me in the car no matter what. We've all heard the cliché "we can do this the easy way or the hard way." but I was going to go in that car and it was incredibly sobering. With the outlandishness of getting arrested for doing something I did not do, I was also trying to process the absolute power these people were welding over me."

His strength and image were not only stripped from him, but his voice was muted as well.

"I didn't see the sheriff again that day, because he went to the local media before my arrest and told them what he was going to do. I found out later on, outside the jail, that all the newspapers and local TV stations were there, and there was an orchestrated press conference. I learned later on the next morning that the judge issued a gag order so that I could not respond, and I would have been liable for any media outlet that published a response. I was put in a cage and I was segregated from the world, while they're putting out their version of what happened. So my friends, my coworkers, the city at large, the county, everyone heard that I did this horrible thing. I had no voice."

The county's pursuit of justice was merely a pursuit to find someone guilty regardless of proof.

Guilty by Corruption

If the accusation of murder by the hands of Michael Morton seemed odd, the claims made about his character at trial were a belligerent bizarre behemoth. Friends and neighbors, all of a sudden, were quick to ding his character and lie under oath about his "troubled" relationship with his wife. It is as if the surging wave of media influence directly controlled the brains of the entire public even some of the people that knew him the best.

When the newspapers and local TV broadcasts asked their audience to jump, the readers and listeners asked how high? But, the true master designers behind this brainwashing propaganda was not the media. Instead it was their sources, Sheriff Jim Boutwell and Williamson County Prosecutor Ken Anderson. They dazzled others with their bursts of fire of indisputable evidence, pulled the levers for smoke screens to keep the public away from the possible truth, and the boom of their voices struck fear into others. These two kept all attention focused on the alleged mastermind murderer at the defense table in the courtroom as if he was the big wizard head in "The Wizard of Oz" while crossing their fingers that no one would pay attention to the men manipulating the evidence behind the curtain.

Michael describes these two men presenting him as "a lower life-form, a sex-mad, selfish monster without redeeming qualities, someone who was clearly and unquestionably guilty." His trial took one absurd turn after another, and important evidence was withheld from him and his defense team of attorneys.

It took almost a quarter of a century later for these important documents and files to surface from the depths of the county and be brought into the light.

Michael's entire life was put on display in that courtroom, and the majority of it was filled with lies. His parents and siblings heard these morbid atrocities and so did Chris' parents and family. Jim Boutwell described him as a man who felt nothing when he discovered the news of Chris' death despite him having felt as if he was falling internally.

There was a lot that was said in the trial, but perhaps the most outlandish accusatory cry came from Ken Anderson when he accused Michael at the witness stand of performing crude sexual acts with Chris' dead body after he had beaten her to death in a porn-fueled rage. This was said in front of a packed courtroom with family, friends, and strangers. His mother heard this about her baby boy.

Chris' mother had to process this image of her daughter's ex-lover. He could not raise a convincing voice against this duo of Butch Cassidy and the Sundance Kid. Instead, he just melted in humiliation with nowhere to turn. After all, how could a monster like Michael respond to these public heroes?

These were the men representing the State. This was the power of the manipulation of the State at its finest. He was guilty until proven innocent.

The guilty verdict caused Michael to collapse in his chair. His thoughts became very self-centered while he waited for the jury to decide on his length of punishment. He turned to his mother-in-law and mouthed to her that he didn't do it. She returned a face of pity and disbelief, and Michael saw that she believed he was lying to her. She shook her head no, and on that rejection, he turned his back to her because he had to focus on the upcoming determination of his prison sentence.

When Michael received his life sentence, he believed that he would have to serve it for life, but he later came to learn that he would be eligible for parole in twenty years. He remembers hearing the cries and shrieks in the courtroom, as well as the way his mother wailed. He briefly embraced his family members and exchanged some sentiments before he was handcuffed again and taken back to the county jail. He was sent to the part of the jail with other inmates who were on their way to the penitentiary.

Michael was officially deemed guilty. There was no hope of returning to society any time soon. He headed off to prison for a very long time. His mentality had to adjust. Yes, he was still grieving Chris, he was still concerned about Eric's well-being, he was still questioning the preposterous thinking of Ken Anderson and Jim Boutwell, he was still processing the label of murderer, but now he had to learn quickly and adjust to prison life with violent inmates at the Texas State Penitentiary in Huntsville, Texas. Survival instincts kicked in right away.

"It was a different mood and mindset. It was a different caliber of

people there. These were not the criminals with misdemeanors. They knew the game. They knew this world. There was an old con, sort of the old shot-caller of the tank, and he knew I had never been to the penitentiary before, and he said to me, "I've been watching you. You should be okay, but I'm telling you when you first get down there keep your mouth shut and your eyes open" and that was some of the best advice I got."

The Caged Bird Doesn't Sing

There is no introductory book to prison life. Each inmate is thrown into the water at once, and only there will to be courageous determines if they sink or swim.

"It doesn't matter if the person was innocent or guilty as sin, prison was a metaphoric machine. They processed people coming in there and it was like clockwork. The prison machine relentlessly grinds on, and inmates are just thrown into it. Inmates react. Inmates can't plan. It's by design, and it happens quickly.

"When I first got there, it was a time with some of the most serious overcrowding, and I didn't go to a cell my first few nights there. I was actually on a bunk out in the hallway on a cell block. Word got out that the federal judge was going to come inspect one of the prisons around Huntsville, and the prison administration didn't know where. So the prison staff got me, and a bunch of other guys out of the hallway, and into a cell. That was the first time I could relax a little bit because when that door closed, there was only one guy in that cell with me. It was different than being out in the hallway where people move around all of the time. Once I got inside, I could take a breath, assess and plan, and try to decide what was next."

This is where he had the first opportunity to reflect on his fate and on who might be the actual killer. Emotions, ideas, and what-if scenarios came flooding into his mind all at once.

"I thought about: What was the real killer doing? Was he even aware that I was arrested? Did he know that there was a trial and that

I was in prison? Could he even read the newspapers, or on the other hand, was he one of these brilliant guys that dodges the cops and evades detection, and I got left holding the bag? I wondered about him. Was this guy trying to get my wife for some reason or was it totally random?"

Michael was able to determine that his wife probably was not targeted for a certain reason through careful reflection of evidence. This provided him with a little sense of peace because he felt Eric was not an upcoming target for this masked murderer. Eric was safe with his relatives, and that kept his spirits intact. He shifted his mindset to his own well-being after his newfound confidence that the most important person in his life was safe.

How did these series of perfectly timed events and testimonials point to him? Why was he paying the price for a crime he did not commit? How would he respond?

"I'm the prodigal son. At that moment in my life, I didn't look to God for fairness or interaction with us, or caring, or maybe, even existing. Part of my adaptation to the penal life was that I learned really quickly there were a whole lot worse things in the world than just getting beat up. I did not back down. I'm not 6'4". I'm not a Golden Gloves boxer. I don't have a black belt in Kung Fu. A lot of guys are not either, they were just like me, but the difference between the people who suffer horribly and the ones that get by, is the matter of their will and how strong they are on the inside. A beating is not the worst thing that can happen to someone by far. Black eyes heal. Busted lips heal."

So, in a life filled with violence and anxiety, Michael found hope in the only thing that kept his spirits up. He believed that he would get out one day and that he would convince Eric that he was not the monster who killed his mother. He discovered that he would be eligible for parole after twenty years even though he was given a life sentence. That love for Eric in his heart kept him going every day although it was quickly overshadowed by the growing rage and desire for revenge. He planned to persuade his son of the truth, and simultaneously plotted his vengeance on his perpetuators.

He knew who was responsible for locking him up, and giving him his life sentence. He watched the county sheriff sit at the witness stand and lie about him. He listened to the prosecutor say outlandish, filthy things about him. He witnessed the medical examiner testify and change the time of death to make him look guilty. Michael had an instinctual desire for revenge, and he became very, very angry. He spent years planning how he was going to kill each and everyone one of them. He kept a list of his targets, and made plans to murder these individuals on different days and in different ways. He was confident that none of these murders would leave a bread crumb trail back to him.

"I had this murder in my heart, and this limitless love for my son. He was what kept me going. That was my life."

Golden Light

Love and avenged murder cannot coexist in a hardened heart at the same time. One will always destroy the other. His moment of brokenness came fourteen years into his sentence.

"I was there for about fourteen years, and I got a letter about my son because he wasn't writing to me at this time. In 2001, he turned eighteen and the letter informed me he was going to legally change his name, and be adopted by the people who were raising him before. My wife's murder, the trial, the conviction, penal life, nothing had ever broken me, but when I legally and officially lost my son ... that was what broke me. I didn't know what to do. I had no idea where to turn, and in a very uncharacteristic moment, I literally cried out to God, "Help, show me something. I got nothing." and when I made that plea, I got nothing in return. I heard an aching silence."

The lack of an immediate answer never means that one is not coming. It's often in the most broken moments that God shines through the brightest. And, when it's an unexpected encounter, it will change a person's life forever.

"At the time when that realization of the aching silence hit me, I wasn't overly shocked or surprised. I had to weigh and consider the arc of my life at that point, and how it was going down and down. I just shrugged it off and trudged on because there was no option. I had to keep going.

"A short while later, maybe a couple weeks, I'm not really sure, but I do know this: it was a very, very average day."

Routine.

"The penitentiary is predictable and repetitive."

Routine.

"I had a normal day."

Routine.

"I didn't eat anything funny. I didn't get hit in the head. But at the end of that day, I was in my cell, and I was in the top bunk. My cellmate was already asleep, and I put on my radio headphones, and turned on my radio to go up and down the dial a couple times and call it a night. This was my evening routine. At this point in 2001, I had done this thousands of nights. I went up and down the dial, and caught a classical station out of Houston and heard a harp. Harp music for me was pretty unusual on the radio. So I listened to it for a moment, and now I think it was comically apropos, that as I stretched out on my bunk I didn't have any warning at all. In just a snap, I found myself bathed in golden light. It was all I could see. Just this wonderful golden light. It was warm, and I felt its warmth. I felt as if I might have been floating over my bunk. I needed no explanation. It was self-evident that I was in the presence of God. He was right there. And above and beyond anything more powerful than anything else, I sensed his limitless and boundless deep, deep, deep love aimed right at me personally. We all hear God loves everybody, and, while that is definitely true, it is very different when it is directed at you. It's personal. I experienced God's individual love for me. And this is how I knew it was real and genuine because something changed inside of me. The next days and weeks while I was trying to understand what happened, I realized that I did

nothing to earn this except ask. Suddenly, I wanted to be better or worthy and I didn't want bad things."

His revolutionary encounter with God shattered his hardened heart that was hell-bent on revenge into a billion pieces. It was replaced and filled with forgiveness for his accusers and enemies.

He makes it very clear during any speech or interview that this was not a "Hallelujah moment," and the gates of the prison did not open the next day filled with cheering inmates and friendly prison guards wishing him luck on his path back to civilized assimilation. He spent another decade in prison and never experienced something like this again. He clung to the genuine change in his heart when doubt tried to seep into his mind about the realness of the experience, or after the other inmates called B.S. after his story. He asked for help in a simple cry to God, and he was answered in a miraculous way that he could not have imagined. But, forgiving people such as Jim Boutwell and Ken Anderson was far from easy.

"I knew I was supposed to forgive those guys, but I didn't want to. But, I knew I was obligated to do that. So I bit the bullet and took a deep breath, and I went to the person on the top of my list, and I consciously, and deliberately forgave them and let that go. That's when I got the surprise because when I did that, I had this very real sense of losing all the weight that had been on me. I felt lighter, cleansed, and healed. I got all of this positive feedback from doing this thing. So, I did it again and worked all the way down my list forgiving these people. Each time I felt better and better.

The forgiveness was about me; it was not about them. We are told to forgive because it helps us. These people didn't know I was coming for them. I forgave them to help myself. I didn't consciously know it at the time, but that's the way it works."

A new Michael Morton was born fourteen years into prison, and he found a new spiritual identity. This lit the path to a new innocent identity in the public eye as well. It was time for him to receive a little help from the Innocence Project.

Getting Life

The Innocence Project is a non-profit organization whose mission is: "to free the staggering number of innocent people who remain incarcerated, and to bring reform to the system responsible for their unjust imprisonment." This would be the only chance Michael had to remove the label of murderer, so he prayed every day for a break through.

One of Michael's attorneys at trial, Bill Allison, was good friends with Berry Scheck, one of the cofounders of the Innocence Project. Michael thought that he had a golden ticket to jump to the front of the line, but the Innocence Project doesn't work that way. The Innocence Project does not operate on favoritism. They have limited assets, and they cannot take every case. They specialize in DNA but they have a budget, and not every case has the evidence or record to get someone exonerated. Many inmates hope to receive their freedom through a false positive on a test. This organization knows that some inmates are just trying to gain the system, so they spend a lot of time separating the wheat from the chaff. It took Michael many years to have his case accepted by the organization.

When Michael finally broke through the first barrier of the process, he was asked if he would feel comfortable with the representation services of John Raley throughout the duration of the process. John was a Houston attorney who had great success in the courtroom. However, his success was in medical malpractice, not in a criminal case. This was John's first criminal trial. Michael described John as a "brawler in court," and he was confident that John would be the best person to fight for him.

Yet, there came a point when no one was sure if the case would move forward due to the lengthy red tape system of the legal process. So, John decided to visit him in Huntsville to peer into his eyes with the hope of detecting the honesty of his soul.

"Because of our little interview, he was convinced I was telling the truth. He went back and talked with his wife and told her that I was innocent, and she said, "Well, John, get him out." He spent the next

117

seven or eight years doing that."

Michael spent every day for eight years with the hope of receiving positive news. But what is a good redemption story without a persistent and pesky villain on the other side? Williamson County refused to cooperate with John and his team. They did not want to turn over files or evidence, particularly a blue bandana that his brother-in-law had picked up near the original murder scene. It clearly could have been dropped by the assailant on his escape route, but this piece of evidence never made it to the courtroom during his original trial along with other important missing files that the prosecution withheld.

The judge finally ruled in John's favor, and they were able to test the bandana with new DNA testing that wasn't available back then. The bandana contained DNA from another man that wasn't Michael's, and it was comingled with his wife's DNA putting someone else at the crime scene. This was huge news, but it wasn't a get-out-of-jail free card because the prosecution, in fact, Ken Anderson's protégé, continued to stall and question the validity of the reasoning behind Michael's innocence.

They ran this mysterious DNA through the database and found that it matched Mark Alan Norwood who had a long criminal history in the California criminal database. That still wasn't enough, so John's team went gold mining for precious files. John's team found a cold case file that was nearly identical to Chris' murder as the prosecution continued to stall. The murder that happened in Austin appeared to have the same modus operandi in regards to the victim; a woman with a small child, the way of the murder, the time of day, and what's really freaky is that it happened on the thirteenth of the month as well. This murder occurred seventeen months into Michael's sentence. This cold case file is what changed the fate of Michael forever. The prosecution could do nothing from that point forward to prevent his exoneration.

Freedom

It was a long road, but Michael finally walked through the prison gates and the county courthouse as a free man on October 4, 2011. He spent nearly twenty-five years of his life behind bars for a murder he did not commit.

"When I saw that things were coming to fruition and I was going to get out, one of my prayers during this whole process was that I wouldn't be overwhelmed by all of the new stuff: the freedom, the colors, female company, the sounds, and all the new stuff. That has been an answered prayer. There's a visual representation on that first day I got out. John Raley was at my elbow helping me along, and we were headed out the door of the courthouse when he turned to me and said, "Michael, breathe freedom." We stepped out the door, and it was a beautiful fall day. The sun was beaming on us, and there was a light breeze. I closed my eyes and I lifted my face up to the sun, and it just felt so good. I didn't realize it, but a guy snapped a picture and John got it, blew it up, and 'posterized' it. It is in his law office today. That embodies that first moment of honest to God freedom. I've been out a little over six years, and it still gets me every time I think of it."

Then, the celebration began in downtown Austin. The team of attorneys put Michael up in a fancy hotel, and he had a dinner filled with rediscovered colors, textures, and tastes at a fancy restaurant. The food was unlike the bland, almost colorless prison fare.

"I remember very specifically that I got to choose some of the things that I wanted to eat, and I got to eat some trout. It was a really nice fish dinner. Also, I remember picking up silverware for the first time in 25 years because I had been using plastic sporks. The silverware seemed wonderfully heavy. It was like riding a bicycle. My so-called table manners came back and I remembered how to use a knife and fork. I was a little bit shaky at first, but I got the hang of it real quickly."

The team at the Innocence Project asked him what he wanted to do after dinner, and he couldn't resist the urge to return to one of his passions from twenty-five-years ago - swimming. He had the chance to be engulfed by the cool pool water as soon as they got back to the hotel. It's hard to imagine the ability to forget how the weight of a fork feels with a piece of steaming fresh trout on the end of it, and it's difficult to envision the recaptured passion inside that results from an absent passion, but he experienced it all again for the first time.

"I hadn't been submerged under water for almost a quarter of century. Swimming is like flying. I remember jumping off the side of that pool and into the water, and I just sailed across the water. It was like being weightless. It was like a second baptism into the free world."

The most fulfilling moment of freedom for Michael came when he saw his son again for the first time. His team of attorneys had a difficult time finding him, but through serendipity and answered prayer, they happened to stumble upon his recent wedding announcement in a local newspaper. Eric was hesitant at first, but he eventually agreed to meet with Michael at John Raley's house. No media. No press. Just a father and a son trying to pick up the broken pieces of lies and wrongful conviction that separated their bond.

"My son showed up with his new wife, and they had been married for about a year. She was about seven or eight months pregnant. While things were not identical, we both had new jeans on, similar styled shirts, and pretty close to identical shoes. In all candor, it was a little awkward, so John saw that and took us to his backyard. There was a large wooden swing in his backyard, and he asked us to sit down, and then he left us. So, my son and I were rocking gently in that swing, and the years slowly started melting away. It was just the sound of our voices. That began our long process of us coming back together. I love him dearly and he loves me. He's given me three grandchildren now.

"That thing I craved all those years in the penitentiary has now come about. I have my son back. He amazes me. Imagine what you would have to do if you had to completely reinterpret who you think you are - what you think you know. He did it. It was a process, and it was tough. He amazes me on so many levels."

Michael dreamed of that day for twenty-five years. He finally had what he prayed for, and it was more than what he could ever ask for. He was a father to Eric once again.

Michael is flourishing today. He is happily remarried and travels the country speaking on large stages to inspire others with his story. He has written an amazing book with pinpoint detail about his journey in <u>Getting Life</u>. He has turned defeat, demoralization, and depression into perseverance, faith, and joy. But, what about those twenty-five years he had to waste in prison? He must feel that the world owes him some debt for his suffering, right?

"I do not wrestle with what happened. We need our trials. The bad things we go through are what makes us. We are told we will have troubles in this world. We need what we're going through. I have to look back and it's a bitter pill, it's a harsh reality, it's tough, but that's what I needed to get where I am today. I don't understand my wife's murder. I'm not all knowing. But, I know that what I went through got me to exactly where I am today."

Throughout his entire story I had one question that continued to knock on the door of my own heart: it's one thing to be stuck in prison, but how do you escape the prison of your own mind? I constantly wrestle with my previous mistakes, and how things could be different now if I didn't make those mistakes. My mind races, reflecting upon the changes that would have resulted in my life if I would have pivoted right instead of pivoting left. And, sometimes I stress over others' preconceived notions and interpretations of my character and integrity. His response to the travesty of injustice was unexpected, yet carefully crafted and sincere from him.

"The only way for you to not get caught in the prison of your mind is to realize that you are not the most important person in the world. Love God with all you got, and love your neighbor as yourself. When you do that and stop being that narcissistic, egotistical, me, me, me guy, then you can get through anything. You can get through hardship, marital problems, money problems … you can get through prison. You take yourself out of the center of the universe, that's it."

Many, many people assumed the worst in Michael Morton. He

went from the stereotypical image of the common man living the American Dream to the most despised figure in his community. He became an outcast, and nearly everyone turned their back on him. Important evidence proving his innocence was withheld from trial. False testimonies scorched his reputation. Two men humiliated an innocent man in their pursuit of political power. His son was ripped from his arms. His voice was powerless. His life consisted of concrete walls, convicts, violence, and loneliness for twenty-five years.

A phoenix rose from the ashes. He became a free man. The people who lied about him were proven wrong, although Ken Anderson should have received a harsher punishment than serving ten days in jail, and forfeiting his law license (he was a judge at the time) for being found guilty of withholding exculpatory evidence. Mark Alan Norwood was found guilty and sentenced to life in prison.

Michael and Eric formed a great relationship. It was a long and ridiculous fight, but he had won as the Underdog versus the State, and gained a much wiser perspective on faith and life in the process. One that he is genuinely thankful for.

CHAPTER 10

Episode 1 - Fighting Cancer
Phil Taylor

The Sea

The Pacific Ocean waves crashed onto the shore as we inhaled a deep breath of cool ocean air at six in the morning. We frantically put on our wetsuits to shield us from the bitter winds of the Seal Beach shore. The morning was frigid in Southern California terms, and we knew what the initial dive into the Pacific Ocean would bring: mostly tense muscles, shortened breaths, racing adrenaline, and goose bumps despite the wetsuits. Yet, we knew that an exhilarating moment of diversion awaited us in those melodic waves.

The sea has a way of extinguishing everything that is troubling back at home. I was in the midst of the most difficult time of my life. My friend, Phil, standing next to me was about to enter the most painful time of his life as well. I was thankful to have him there like a brother by my side. We picked up our surfboards together and raced to the water without knowing what the future held.

Plato, the famous Greek philosopher, said, "The sea cures all ailments of man." My skin felt numb from the cold water, and I shivered any time the wind whipped across my face. However, that water provided a temporary respite from my continuous worried heart while I sat on that surfboard about thirty yards offshore. Those hours of riding the waves on our surfboards are stitched into my memory, because it was a time of joy before everything quickly slipped downhill for both of us.

Phil mentioned a discomfort in his stomach when we arrived back to my apartment. It was not the first time it had happened. The sun had just risen high enough to begin waking up sleepy Saturday Southern California residents. We felt rejuvenated like it was already high noon, and we had been up for hours talking about "solving" the world's problems. But, his ailment raised my own internal red flag. My buddy generally was not one to complain about anything, and his second statement about his stomach pain over the past twenty-four hours left me wondering what could be wrong. He walked into the bathroom in the apartment and spent a long time in there. When he walked out, I could sense that he was not suffering from the normal stomach bug that comes and goes. He was in tremendous pain, and he passed some awful waste matter and more.

"Whoa, there buddy! What happened in there?!" I said, trying to laugh it off for him.

"Yeah, I don't feel so good," he half-heartedly responded. "I'm in some pain, and it kind of feels like something is blocking my digestive system."

"You should definitely go get that checked out, even though I'm sure it's fine. Better safe than sorry."

"I will. Once I get back home to Texas, I will."

Again, this was strange. He was never one to complain about anything. We met at Texas Christian University where we both played on the football team. He was an extremely likeable guy, and I would bet you that Betty White has a better chance of knocking out Chuck Norris with a roundhouse kick to his jaw line than for you to find someone who didn't like Phil. However, the most probable reason why we bonded so well during our football days was because he was a wide receiver, and I was a quarterback.

We were definitely not "stars" on the team. In fact, we were walkons and didn't get many reps in practice outside of scout team, but that didn't prevent us from meeting up numerous times outside of scheduled practices, or staying late after practice to run routes, or teaming up for extra workouts in the weight room. Our friendship grew outside of the white lines on the field due to our quality time spent with each other around the football facilities and on campus. He was dedicated. He knew how to put his head down and work hard. Never once during my college career, did I ever hear him complain in the 105 degree weather during a "Colorado" leg workout which entailed a lot of running and agility drills after barbell squatting, and left our muscles shaking like Jello. Nor did he show stereotypical wide-receiver prima donna syndrome if I threw him an inaccurate pass or threw it to a different receiver.

He had always been immune to voicing discomfort and chuckled off any weight-lifting or muscle aches with, "It's not that bad." But this stomach pain felt beyond bad for him, and he was telling me about it.

Underdog Roots & Brotherhood

Phil grew up in beautiful Foothill Ranch, Southern California in Rick Warren (the world-renown pastor of Saddleback Church) country near Rick's notorious Saddleback Church Lake Forest campus. Phil's family is one-of-a-kind, and his parents, Bret and Myra, are the incredible Christian parents that other parents attempt to emulate. I visited his parents at his home when I had some extra time after a work trip in May 2018. His hallway to his bedroom is filled with awards and recognition of community service and athletics throughout his career at Orange Lutheran High School and at TCU. Bret and Myra gleam when they call it the "Hall of Fame".

He grew up playing sports and within his Christian faith. He was constantly recognized as the hardest worker and the most dedicated Christian on the team. He lacked Division I football size and stature and, simply put, was an underdog attempting to play football in college. He was five foot ten inches tall and weighed 190 pounds at his max at TCU. Yet, what he lacked in size, he made up in heart and hustle. The guy could "straight up" play football and could catch anything that I threw his way. If I tossed him a football, a tennis ball, an egg, or a wrench, like in the movie, "Dodgeball," then he would gather in the pass with concentrated dexterity and tuck it away gently under his arm like he was holding his own child before he turned up field and ran right by a defender.

I've even heard from multiple sources that he never dropped a ball in high school that touched his hands. He knew that his path to collegiate athletics was through a walk-on opportunity even though he had hands like glue, and the credibility of playing on one of the best high school teams in California. Underdogs, those people with small stature and big hearts and bigger drive, have a certain mindset from the get-go when they aspire to accomplish their goals. Determination and faith was all that he needed to earn his position on the squad. His heart drew him to Texas, and he set off for Texas Christian University in 2011.

Phil and I became friends quickly when I transferred into TCU from another school in 2012. Throughout all of our practices and drills together, I don't remember him dropping one pass. Again, he was an underdog by a long shot to ever play during game day. The coaching staff at TCU recruits some of the fastest, quickest, strongest, and most athletic talent in the country, and the wide receiver position usually has the deepest depth chart. The glory of stepping on the field during play on game day may have never come his way, but he never overlooked his opportunity. He considered a position on the TCU football team as the highest honor he could attain. The majority of the public never knew of his forty hour per week commitment to blood, sweat, agonizingly hard work, and tears throughout the school year. He did not care. He knew he was blessed and had been given the opportunity almost every pop warner and high school football player dreams of every day. So, he wore a smile every day and chose to encourage teammates, rather than complain.

Phil didn't receive any playing time until his last year in 2014 when the Horned Frogs went on to win the "Chik-fil-a Peach Bowl" in

Atlanta against Ole Miss. He was called into the game during the last game of the regular season at home against Iowa State University, and he had a play called for him. He lined up on the left side of the field in the slot receiver position, motioned over to the quarterback before the snap and then took a jet sweep shuffle pass around the right side of the field weaving through traffic for a five-yard gain before a defender dragged him to the ground.

For me, it was like watching the climactic ending of the movie "Rudy", but on your favorite stretch of 100 yards. It was a great play and the topic of many conversations for us after that. All of the hard work that he put into a team effort without a scholarship had come to fruition in that five-yard sprint. The underdog within him had beaten the odds he was given to play college football. He proudly earned a first down for his team which was one of the best in the country that year.

Fast forward to late 2016, and I was in the midst of the most difficult time of my life. I was drowning in depression, anxiety, hopelessness, and pain.

Phil's little brother was playing in his last high school football game at Orange Lutheran High School, so Phil came to visit. He invited me to join him during the game and spend some time with him, so I could be distracted from everything that was consuming me. Later on, he listened to me spill my guts and crushed spirit to him for hours. In that moment, he was my brother, and he was by my side. His listening and advice meant the world to me. I'll never forget it.

That Devil - the "C" Word

Phil left for the airport after our surfing expedition and followed up with a doctor within a couple of weeks after returning to Texas. Within a month, the doctors discovered that he had a tumor obstructing the flow of his digestive system in his large intestine.

Phil had stage three colon cancer.

"I was diagnosed with colorectal cancer on December 7th, 2016.

127

I was twenty-four-years old. It was bizarre for someone my age to be coming down with this serious issue. It's shocking to be associated with that term."

No family history of the disease. No alcoholic past. No smoking. No genetic predisposition. Nothing. This happened out of nowhere.

This ex-Division I athlete, Brazilian Jujitsu trainee, and health-conscious twenty-four- year old man had the diagnosis of an over-weight fifty-year-old placed on a branch in the midst of a family tree covered with a long history of familial colon cancers. How does one process that? How does one make sense of that news at twenty-four, and with an entire life ahead?

Phil must have been asking the same question that I was asking myself in my own dark situation, "Why God? Why did you allow this to happen? Why me?"

Yet, he didn't react as you may guess. He liked to say, *"If anyone watches their soap operas or their TV dramas, and some character gets diagnosed with cancer, there's always an intense, emotional moment like the girl leaning up against a wall and crying as she slides down it. I knew right away that something was up because the doctor who performed my colonoscopy told me beforehand that he expected to see this or to see that, and they gave me some medication to take care of it, but when all of the other physicians that were a part of the procedure were coming in to talk to me and to check on me, it was kind of strange. So, right away, I knew something was up, and then, the doctor came back and said, 'I found this tumor, and nothing is confirmed, but I've seen this before, and it's going to be cancerous.'*

"I don't think it really hit me at first because my very first thought process was literally, 'well, that sucks'. I don't think it really hit me until maybe a week later. I understood what he was saying, but, at the time, I guess, I didn't really comprehend how big or how life-changing that would be to hear those words. My next thought was when I asked the doctor, 'what do I have to do to get rid of this?' I'm not really a guy who freaks out about things. It was not the best news to hear, but I was not devastated when I heard the news. Maybe at the time I didn't

realize how big of a task it was going to be to get rid of it. My thought process was, 'okay, it's a thing. I got this, but let's move forward and how do I get rid of this?'"

Phil began a new fight as a different type of underdog in December 2016. The arena was different. The opponent was more intimidating than a big linebacker. But he still had his fighting underdog spirit. The match began with a few months of radiation and many doctor visits. He moved in with his Uncle Mike and his Aunt Sheri in a suburb outside of Dallas, but no part of this life-change kept him from his hobbies. Cancer did not define him or the way he went about his life. He continued working and filming games for TCU athletics, the Dallas Mavericks, and the Texas Rangers. He had been involved with sports ever since he could remember. He viewed sports as a great release and escape from the stressors of life, and his opportunity to continue on in a career with sports television was a little kid's dream come true.

He experienced many different emotions when he was alone and behind closed doors the first few months.

"I had my moments. I think it's completely natural and completely normal to have those moments. I tell people when they get bad news it is very good, natural, and healthy to have those emotions. They have to get angry. They have to be sad. That's completely normal, but they can't stay there, and they can't linger on those emotions. At some point, they have to realize, 'okay, I have to move forward because if I stay put, that's not going to get anything done.' I still have my moments of frustration. I try not to ask myself this question too much, 'why? Why me?' I was a twenty-four-year old former college athlete, and I had picked Brazilian jiu-jitsu for a physical fitness regimen, and I was in the best shape of my life. It wasn't like I was smoking cigarettes every day. I was exercising. I was eating right and bam, I just got hit with this."

He continued to spend time with his friends on Friday and Saturday nights in Fort Worth. He would dance at "Billy Bob's Texas," which is the largest country bar in the world. No one could match his skill, rhythm, or smoothness in the two-step. When he didn't feel like dancing, he would spend the evenings watching movies with friends, or playing the FIFA soccer video game into the early hours of the morning with old college roommates. Even though everyone knew what he was facing, he never had a sob story and simply decided to live in the moments that he had been given.

He was always filled with positivity whenever we spoke on the phone together before his surgery in May 2017. Every time I tried to poke him with tough questions about his perspective on his future, he simply responded that his faith had everything figured out. He didn't know how it would all play out, but he knew with unwavering confidence that God would be glorified in the best or worst outcome. He looked toward the future with hope and tried not to live in the memories of his past life before his diagnosis.

"I look back at where I was three years ago, and I tell myself 'dang, I would love to go back to that.' I'd love to still be able to do the things that I was able to do. How do I keep myself from going back? It's just keep moving forward and don't look in the rearview mirror. If I had a chance to go back to that type of health that I was in, then I would do so in a heartbeat, absolutely. But, these are the cards that I was dealt, and I have to play the hand that I was dealt. I don't really have any regrets about the choices that I have made. If I had done something to physically bring this upon me, then I think that would be a lot harder to accept, but it just happened out of the blue. I just focus on what's in front of me and what's ahead of me. The two things that anyone can control is their attitude and their effort. Everything else, other than that, is out of one's control. They can't do anything about it."

During that time, my voice expressed the same words, but I'm not sure if my heart completely meant it. I was still heartbroken about how my own life was unfolding, but now one of my best friends had cancer, too. My mind seemed to be in a never-ending prison sentence, trapped with the good and bad memories of the recent past that seemed to weld together into one endless nightmare.

I never stopped believing that God existed, but I did think to myself: "God, in the Bible it says that you care about us. But, do you really? Because I don't believe you do right now. Do you see what's going on down here? You have the power to heal. Why are you not doing so? Why are you not fighting for me when I'm trying to fight for you? Why are you allowing Phil to suffer like this? Why did this have to happen? How can you possibly claim to be good and know what is best for us?"

The First Discovery

Radiation and chemotherapy became two companions, and simultaneously, two enemies of Phil for the next few months. The oncologist's plan was to shrink the tumor to a manageable level and then remove the tumor from his intestine. He still held his head high, even during this time of his feeling sick. He felt all energy drained out of his body during and after treatment.

Radiation treatment didn't bother him too much. He only felt a lack of energy after treatment. However, he didn't enjoy chemotherapy at all, but he didn't mind the painful side effects of the chemo if it gave him a chance to survive.

All preparation work and radiation before surgery was a success, and Phil was optimistic for a successful surgery. The MRI scans showed that the radiation treatments were effective and shrunk the tumor in his large intestine. It wasn't a drastic change in size, but it was enough for the doctor's to feel confident about surgery.

The plan was to open him up, remove the large tumor, and then connect his large intestine back together so that he could regain normal digestive function. If they were unable to connect the large intestine back together, then they would perform a colostomy in which he would live life with a bag on the outside of his body connected to his large intestine through a hole in his abdominal wall called a stoma. This would collect any waste passing through him for an undetermined amount of time, maybe even forever. Surprisingly, he wasn't nervous going into the surgery. He was just ready.

"I was absolutely ecstatic that the surgeons could get rid of this. Was I excited about the after-effects and the recovery? - No, but in my mind, it was totally worth it to get back to living a normal life. When the doctor said, 'let's do the surgery', I was ecstatic. I was thrilled. I was very excited, and ready to go."

Ready for cancer to be over. Ready for alleviation of pain. Ready for relief of the frustration caused by the dysfunction of the digestive system. Ready for respite from his constant appointments and treatments. Ready to beat cancer once and for all.

Many people who knew Phil tried to place themselves in his shoes and surmised that they would be angry at God for placing this burden on them at such an early age. In fact, most people were already upset at God, because Phil was the least deserving person of this hardship.

"One of the biggest questions that people ask me is, 'why are you not mad at God? You're a twenty-four-year old in great shape, and you have cancer.' That thought never really crossed my mind, which is strange I found out later, because that's not a normal reaction. The cancer was random. In my mind, I'm thinking something good is going to come out of this one way or another. God is going to use this for His glory and His benefit and something good is going to happen. I don't know what. I don't know when. But, at some point there's going to be a positive that comes out of this whole experience. I have gone through worse things than this. I can suck it up, and we can get to the surgery. I have to thank God for putting me in a position where I can have these great doctors, and have an amazing support group of friends and family.

"My prayer to God has always been, 'let them see you, through me.' People come up to me, and they say, 'you are always smiling, and you go through this with such a positive attitude, how do you do that?' I want the answer to be, 'to lead to God.' That's where I get this confidence from. I think getting mad at God is totally okay because I think He's definitely big enough to handle it. I'm not trying to condemn or to put people down when they receive bad news and their first reaction is to say, 'why God?' I'm not trying to put that down at

all. That's just not how my mind works."

His optimism never ceased, at least in front of me. I drove up from Austin on that day in May to be with him before and after his surgery in Dallas. Myra, Sheri, and a couple of good friends were there to wish him well. He had the biggest smile on his face while he sat in the hospital bed with multiple IVs in his arms. He had made it to this day, and he looked forward to the future.

Toward the end of the surgery the doctor came out and told Myra and Sheri the news. First, the good news. They had successfully removed the large tumor from his large intestine. The discovery of multiple flat layered tumors on his abdominal wall was the bad news. The lead surgeon decided to not attach his large intestine back together because of the fear of an immediate return of cancer growth that would lead to another large tumor blocking the digestive tract.

Instead, Phil received a colostomy. But the real shocking news was the presence of these flat tumors on his abdominal wall. They were undetectable from an MRI report, so he and his family had no warning that this could have been a discovery during surgery. Myra was told that these tumors had no cure and were only "maintainable". The cancer had metastasized, and he progressed to an incurable stage four colon cancer.

Myra broke down. Her world continued to crumble beneath her like every step of faith she took was greeted by a darker and deeper sinkhole. She cried in my arms for a long time, and we didn't exchange any words or hopeful pleasantries. All of the family and friends just stood there trying to comprehend this new update.

Most people didn't know at that time the depth of pain that Myra was experiencing within her family. Her husband, Bret, had recently been in the hospital for an extended time for a terrible sinus infection that had been a huge health scare. It had such an effect on him, that he was unable to be at Phil's surgery because he simply could not handle the change in altitude pressure that comes with flying, so he remained at home in California. On top of this, Myra was dealing with the combined emotions of stress and joy that come with a wedding. Her daughter was preparing to get married in Nebraska within the next thirty days. And, this is just the despised icing on the cake, Myra had her own health scare a few weeks after Phil's surgery when the doctor found a lump on her breast. She had been diagnosed with breast cancer. Fortunately, they caught it very early on, so it never became a serious or prolonged threat.

"My Mom has been awesome and has been a rock. I can't imagine having one of my own kids halfway across the country get diagnosed with cancer and having them be all by themselves. That would be really brutal. A few weeks after my surgery, we found out that she was diagnosed with stage zero breast cancer and didn't tell anyone, but Dad. It was more of a safety thing, and they went in and cut out the area that they thought could potentially turn cancerous.

"She's always smiling and always ready to love on her kids. It's been really neat to have her fly out to Texas to spend time with me. Mom has been great and very supportive. She is always doing mom things like sending texts, sending cookies, and she's an arts and crafts wizard so she'll crochet beanies and scarves, and stuff like that for me."

Take a breath right now and put yourself in the shoes of that mother. Try to compartmentalize your own diagnosis, your husband's illness, your son's surgery discovery, and your daughter's upcoming celebration. Can you even do it? Would you even have the energy to lift your head up? Yet, that's exactly what she did. After her tears stopped, and a few coughs to clear her throat were let out, she looked up at me while continuing to give me a big bear hug and said, "God has a plan. We must continue to have faith, no matter what."

What? Um, hello, did you hear what the doctor just said? This new "diagnosis" wasn't even a consideration before surgery, and now all Phil could do was hope the doctors could maintain his cancer. How could the mother of Phil respond like that when I couldn't even respond with a coherent sentence? The answer is due to her rock-solid faith in Jesus. She was going to believe that this season of turmoil had purpose, and that it was only temporary in the grand scheme of an eternal perspective. There was nothing that was going to tear her faith apart, not even cancer.

On the other hand, I had a really difficult time seeing God's goodness in any of this. I had hit rock bottom emotionally, and the news of Phil's new cancer threat had felt like the dirt that was being tossed on me to bury me in the ditch. It felt like the dirt would continue to pile on and pack me in no matter how much I fought to get out of that ditch. The desire to fight back was absent. Hope was pointless. I was at a serious crossroads of how to view faith in my life. Honestly, I was too tired, perplexed, and hurt to figure it out. I was done.

The Second Discovery

When Phil awoke from surgery, he was informed of the successful removal of the tumor in his large intestine and the consequential colostomy. However, the doctor did not mention the flat layered tumors, because he thought it was best to give him twenty-four hours to recover first. I had the opportunity to visit with him after the doctor gave the clearance. He looked like he had just gone toe-to-toe with Muhammad Ali for twelve rounds, but as usual, he wore a smile on his face. Our conversation was mostly filled with, "I feel like crap," and "I'm going to get really good at video games", yet he did seem slightly satisfied to know that he happened to be the only patient on that floor in the hospital. He had the entire nursing staff waiting for his beckoned call.

From Dallas, I took off to Houston with a heavy heart for work meetings the next day. I could not comprehend what life was trying to iron out. I don't remember much on that long I-45 drive, but I do remember hearing the song "Broken Things" by Matthew West for the first time on the radio, and it gave me a sense of peace and calm that would have otherwise been absent that night.

The news hit Phil hard the next day. His hope for an end to this fight was picked up and punted to the far end of the field. His new outlook left him feeling like he had to carry the football 100 yards to

135

score but had to get by the 1985 Chicago Bears, the 2002 Tampa Bay Buccaneers, and the 1975 Pittsburgh Steelers defense by himself all at the same time.

"My doctor said the cancer is a cause for concern. The cancer is stage four, meaning it has gone from one organ to another. He used terms like, 'this is manageable. It's probably not curable, but we think we can manage it. We can keep going and we can do the best we can to attack this thing.' That hurt. I'm not going to lie, that really hurt to hear that. To go from, I'm going to feel like crap for a month while I recover from surgery, but then I'll get back to a normal life by November, to the battle is still going, and it might not be curable ... that absolutely killed me hearing that. I was already hurting from the surgery recovery, so when you feel bad and you hear bad news, everything is amplified. Hearing that news really gutted me.

"I got pissed. Oh, yeah, I was very angry. Although what's curious is where I was directing my anger. It wasn't at God, and it wasn't at the doctors. It was really at my body, and I literally remember saying, 'I hate you, I bleeping hate you.' That's how I was releasing my emotion at the time because I've always had health issues. My body has not been very nice to me over the years. I think I was angry for about an hour and a half, two hours, and then I was good."

After he let these emotions come and pass, he once again laced up his cleats and was determined to get down that field into the end zone. He lifted all of our spirits because he chose to lift his spirit and decided to trust the process.

The next plan of action called for more aggressive and more frequent chemotherapy with one week on and one week off. And mixed within that regimen, would be scattered treatments of radiation. The ultimate goal was a successful "chemo wash" to wipe out all remaining cancer cells. A chemo wash consists of opening up the abdomen and removing any tumors that the surgeon can see, and then pouring hot liquid chemo in the abdomen to "swish" in all of the cracks and crevices around the organs. The hot liquid chemo should kill all of the cancerous cells that the doctor cannot remove from surgery. It's a daunting surgery to look forward to, that is, assuming that he would even make it to that point.

"I'm definitely not quitting. I tell people I literally have nothing better to do than to get better. I'm down to do whatever it takes at this point. They put a meta-port in the left side of my chest which is a device that looks like a cylinder and has a rubber top. The nurses connect a needle to the meta-port which connects to my veins. I get plugged in. When I go in for chemotherapy infusions, instead of them destroying my arms every time, they have access through my chest. When they give me those pain meds, I feel it instantly, and it is awesome.

"I'm still doing chemo, and I go in every other Monday to a clinic here in Dallas, and I get plugged in for four or five hours. Then I take home a portable pack for forty-six hours or so, and then I get disconnected. The drugs have had some pretty, crazy side effects. I've had neuropathy in my hands, and my hands feel like they're asleep constantly. For the first week and a half after chemo, it's painful to touch or drink cold items. I have a cold aversion which is an absolute joke, because when I started this, it's summertime in Texas, and I can't drink cold things. I need to stay hydrated, because they removed a big chunk of my large intestine which absorbs fluids. So, I have to constantly drink, but I have to drink warm to hot stuff during a Texas summer to stay hydrated, so it's something I laugh about. It's kind of a cruel joke.

"I was dealing with some pretty bad nausea, but the doctors at UT Southwestern have found ways for me to get around it. I have a colostomy which is weird, but it is better than where I was a year ago. The most recent side effect comes from a drug called Vectibix which is a blocker that blocks the signals from my brain to the tumors to stop them from growing. The problem is that it makes me look like I'm sixteen because I'm breaking out with a rash and acne all over my face and my chest."

Chemotherapy picked up, but Phil didn't slow down at all. He continued to work during "off" chemotherapy weeks, and continued to mentor and coach football at Prince of Peace Christian School as an assistant coach. There was no chance that he was going to miss his sister's wedding, so he made the trip to Nebraska and celebrated her new chapter of life. He even made a trip half-way around the world to visit his brother who was serving in the Air Force and stationed in Japan.

The chemo took a much more noticeable effect this time around. He dropped weight, and the concoction of drugs had some adverse side effects that he described before. He chose to look at the good instead. He didn't lose his hair. His family and friends stayed close. And, the colostomy provided a huge relief of pressure and pain from his life for which he was very thankful. He gave credit to his support group that surrounded him.

"I couldn't imagine going through this alone. That would be brutal. So, having people I can talk to, people I can vent to, people who encourage me, it is all super uplifting. I had a friend of mine send me a video with a guy, who talks about complainers, and he says, 'Do you know that every year in the world, two million people will die from dehydration? So now, take a step back, and take a look at your own life. Whether you think your cup is half empty or half full, guess what ... there's still water in it, so drink it and stop complaining.' That hit me, and I thought to myself, 'yep, somebody's always got it worse'. That's my mindset. I go to these infusions and I see a lot of older people who lost their hair, or they have tumors growing out the side of their face. Prior to the Vectibix that caused my face to be all dry and rashy, no one would have an idea that I am going through this physically. I'm walking around and being active. No one would have an idea that I was going through this, and now I look at other people's crazy side effects, and my situation could be totally worse."

These were the cards he was dealt, and he was going to play the best hand that he could. He always found a way to find the blessings in his scenario rather than focusing on the discomforts.

The TCU football program honored Phil in a true family-like

fashion. Our university may not be as big as the University of Florida or Arizona State University, but it is a strong, tight-knit family, one that rivals any atmosphere you may find on another college campus. The news of his continued fight and underdog mentality spread throughout the Dallas-Fort Worth metroplex, and the TCU football program decided to honor his fight in the best way they knew how. He was named an honorary captain on November 21, 2017 when the Horned Frogs hosted the University of Texas Longhorns under a warm Texas sky. He walked out arm-and-arm with his old teammates and stood at the center of the fifty-yard line for the coin toss. The crowd erupted with cheering and applause when he was announced. His smile shone big and bright like the stars deep in the heart of Texas. The Frogs went on to obliterate the nation's most notorious university 41-17 in a packed Amon G. Carter stadium.

Phil is not one to brag or call attention to himself, so he barely talked about it before and after the game, but I know it meant more to him than I can imagine. I've been an observer of a lot of TCU football games both on the field and in the stands, and that was the greatest moment to ever take place on that historic field of grass in my opinion.

Give Him Rest from This

April 2018 quickly approached, and Phil was anxious for the chemo wash surgery. He was slightly nervous about the recovery process that lay ahead, but he was mostly excited about a hopeful end to this seventeen-month fight, even though he may lose multiple organs during the procedure. The doctors were going to open him up and remove all tumors that they could get to, and they were going to remove any non-essential organs that the cancer was growing on.

"The doctors will remove whatever they can get. Then they'll heat up liquid chemotherapy to 105 degrees and they'll dump it into my gut. They'll literally just fill up the crevices and the spaces. Then they'll

139

swish me around for about an hour and a half, and then they'll drain it. Hopefully that chemo will kill off any of the tumors they cannot get through surgery. That is the plan."

Phil's and my good friend, Cobie, and I awoke early and left Irving to make the short drive to UT Southwestern Medical Center in Dallas to be with Phil before his six in the morning surgery. We were told by his family that he had a difficult time sleeping the night before due to pain, and was not in the mood to see any visitors before the surgery when we arrived. We were disheartened, but completely understood his wishes at the same time. This actually gave us the opportunity to have a great conversation with Bret, Myra, and Sheri. Bret was healthy now, and was able to make the trip this go-around, so it was the first time that Cobie and I had the chance to talk to the entire immediate family in depth about Phil's journey.

And, we happened to have the blueprint of this journey at our fingertips. The Fort Worth Star Telegram newspaper released a long article about Phil's battle and placed it as the main feature on their front page on the day of the surgery. It was perfect timing, and the necessary steps it took to get this story printed was miraculous. His friend works for the Star Telegram and interviewed him only a week before the story broke. Everyone on the press team, including the editor, worked on the project in unison with all gears clicking to get this story edited and published by the day of this pivotal procedure. We laughed, sighed, and fought back tears during the reminiscing and could not believe the impact that Phil and his story was making on others. Yet, through the trip down a sad memory lane with his family, it was clear that there was a burning flame of hope in their eyes, but that hope-defying news from the doctors after the surgery was a legitimate concern that they had. A family's life direction hung on the outcome of this surgery.

About forty-five minutes passed before we received delightful news. Phil was given some pain meds and some fluids for his preparation for surgery, and it had completely reversed his spirits. He wanted to see us. When Cobie and I finally got to his bedside, he was all smiles. He was happy to see us, and thankful that we made the trip. We laughed as he told us about how good the drugs were making him feel, and how he wished that he always felt this ready for life-altering surgery. We wished him well, and left the room hastily as the oncologist arrived on the scene to speak with him and mark off the last items on his pre-surgery checklist. Cobie left for work, and I left to make the I-35 drive back home to Austin. I hoped beyond all else, that the flame I saw in his parents' eyes would be burning bright after surgery and instead, would not leave an ascending line of smoke as evidence of a hope that once was.

The surgeon removed four organs from Phil - the gall bladder, appendix, spleen, and a chunk of the liver, because they were all covered with over-reactive cells. In addition, they scraped off more cancerous spots from his intestines and any other place that they could find a clump of the aggressive cells. Overall, the removal of his organs and the wash were deemed a success. He faced a very long road to recovery, but the doctors were confident that they had removed as much as they could, and that this could be a turning point for the better in his fight.

I didn't speak with him immediately after the surgery, because he was too tired to talk, but I did confer with Myra and Sheri a lot. He was in quite a bit of pain after the surgery, but he was excited for the future. When I asked him during the podcast about his thoughts about the upcoming chemo wash, he replied, *"I might lose my spleen. Oh well. Jason Witten lost his spleen and he is still in the NFL, so I think I'll be okay."* He solely focused on the end of this fight. He saw the light at the end of the tunnel and just wanted to get there, no matter the route chosen. So, he didn't overreact like one might expect when the doctors informed him of all of the organs that they removed. He knew it was part of this drawn-out process. His objective was to finish recovery, and return to a normal life with or without certain organs. He was as happy as can be, given the circumstances. His spirit was far from broken.

Unending

"The best-case scenario is that the wash would let me live without chemo. That would let me live normally and then maybe every year or two years they would perform another "camera check" to see if it is growing back. Stage four cancers don't ever really go away. They can contain them, but it's not really going to ever go away. My surgeon described the process as resetting the clock. If I do these scans every year or so, and they realize the cancer is coming back, then they can open me up, do another wash, and reset it. That's the best-case scenario. In the worst-case scenario, I didn't respond to the chemo which would not be ideal. I would probably look into some trials and try some other drugs. We're hoping that it doesn't come to that, but if it does, then we'll just deal with it. I'm down for whatever works at this point."

A couple of weeks after his release from the hospital he was re-admitted into the concrete walls of wondering what the next news will be. The doctors and nurses put multiple drains and plugs in Phil, because "things" were leaking on the inside. This also included a catheter. He hated this, and I could tell from our brief conversations and his family's updates, that this was the most frustrating part of this fight. He didn't blink an eye at chemo. He didn't mind his colostomy bag. But, these drains did not sit well with him, and he never had a break from them. This nuisance was only magnified in the coming weeks when his scheduled appointments to remove the drains were only met with doctor's orders that he had to keep them in because he still needed them.

This frustration and pain was followed by another defeat. A routine scan a month removed from his surgery revealed cancerous growth on his diaphragm. The cancer was back, and it was back much sooner than anyone expected. He knew that the cancer could return, but everyone expected that it would take place many months after the surgery if it were to happen at all. He was clogged up with drains in places they didn't belong, still recovering from the removal of four organs and having poison dumped into every crack and crevice of his abdomen, stuck in a hospital from which he couldn't escape, and the cancer was back. The nightmare continued to intensify and presented a frightening shadow of terror at the turn of every chapter.

How would he ever win this fight?

Nosedive

It was a joyous occasion on the day that Phil finally had the drains removed. His joy didn't last long, however, because he was put back on chemo and radiation shortly after. They increased the dosages with the hope of maintaining the cancer. A cure was not scientifically possible. The only hope that we all had was for a miracle of healing to take place.

Family and friends had witnessed him battle cancer for one and a half years. This was the first time that I can honestly say that I saw a change in his demeanor. The large reservoir of hope that once was full had significantly evaporated. I don't think he felt he had the enthusiasm to carry on this fight. Some of his friends noticed the decline in his spiritual and emotional health in addition to his rapid weight loss. My friend, Marissa, shared with me during one conversation, "This go-round has been much tougher on Phil than anything we have seen before. I can see it breaking him down." It was true. He still presented a skip in his step, but it was off-beat. He still carried a smile, but it wasn't meant to light up the room.

He never tried to draw attention to himself, yet he was battling the demon of fear and doubt that none of us wanted to confront ourselves. Everyone wanted to encourage him, yet the risk of meaningless words falling on deaf ears often kept us reserved to ourselves. What do you say to a friend whose fate is clearer than yours, and how do you even bring up the subject?

Phil began making trips to MD Anderson in Houston, which is one of the world's most renowned hospitals for cancer treatment, to get a second opinion, and explore clinical trial options. He eventually agreed upon a clinical trial taking place in San Antonio that required him to drive every Sunday to San Antonio for Monday morning treatments. His underdog mentality was badly bruised and beaten, but it still existed. Life had become more daunting and he continued to decide to push on, whether in full spirit or partial spirit.

He continued to coach football at Prince of Peace Christian School just outside Dallas. His passion for the offensive side of the line of scrimmage shined bright, but it was outmatched by his devotion to form relationships with his players and teach them a few things about life outside of the football field. His love of sports and endless pursuit to live life to the fullest, was fully on display.

Phil and I had plans to meet up during the first few weeks of the 2018 TCU football season. We were going to go to the TCU vs. Ohio State game in AT&T Stadium in week three of the college football season. However, I found out that day he had been readmitted into the hospital due to his pain and swelling in his abdomen. Marissa went to visit him the day after the game, and she called me after and shared, "Phil does not look good. He looks the worst I've seen him yet. He is the skinniest I've ever seen him. The doctors and I agree that we would be shocked if he made it to Christmas."

The following weekend he was supposed to meet me in Austin, Texas for the TCU vs. Texas game. He spent more time than expected in the hospital, and the fluid build-up in his lungs prevented him from any form of travel when he was released. I was hugely disappointed to miss him two weeks in a row, but I had grown accustomed to his frequent hospital trips. After all, there was nothing that he could do, or that I could do, to change it.

On the Sunday evening after the TCU vs. Texas game, I still had not heard from Phil, so I called his Uncle Mike to ask how Phil was feeling. Mike told me that all of Phil's siblings flew to Dallas to spend the weekend with him. Deep concern raised itself in my mind, and I asked Mike to elaborate further. Phil's health declined progressively over the past seven days, and especially within the past forty-eight hours. No one expected it over the preceding weeks, but Phil was on an irreversible nose-diving descent that was headed straight to the ground.

"Mike, I am already planning to come visit him this upcoming weekend. Should I keep those plans, or should I come sooner than that?" I asked.

"I would get here as fast as you can. We set up hospice this weekend at our house. We don't know what is going to happen," he replied.

I drove up the next day not knowing what to expect when I reached Mike and Sheri's driveway. Mike met me out front, and gave me the latest update that left my heart in my throat. Myra, family, and friends were inside with more people on the way. Bret was in a hospital in downtown Dallas the last couple of days and was still there. Bret could not leave the hospital, because he was battling a heart virus that the doctors had to closely monitor. But, even though Bret was in the hospital, the family was giving all of their attention to Phil.

Phil had less than twenty-four hours left to live, and Phil knew it.

Our Father

I was breathless and numb when I saw my buddy resting on a recliner in the living room. The Phil I had known was not the frail skeleton that sat on the chair before me. My buddy was almost unrecognizable. He woke up when I sat down and began to speak to him. I instantly saw the attitude I knew and loved when I looked into his eyes, and I believe I saw his soul. He was happy to see me, although he continued to fade in and out of consciousness. He would stay awake for twenty seconds, and then fall asleep for a few minutes. He was heavily medicated with pain medicine administered by the hospice nurse every hour, on the hour. While he was awake, he spoke, although it was difficult to understand all that he was saying. Fortunately, someone in the group of friends and family that surrounded him always understood him, and he expressed how happy he was that I came to visit and say goodbye.

I sat there next to him for the next twenty minutes wanting to tell him so many different things while not knowing what to say at all. It was the greatest paradox of my life. How do you begin the last

145

conversation with your best friend?

Finally, after the superficial and awkward conversation ended, I took my friend's hand, and with a deep breath, I surveyed the face of my friend who had fallen back asleep on his recliner. I studied the features of his face, the lack of warmth in his hands, and the way his chest fought to gather air with each passing breath. I summoned up the courage to share with him what was on my heart, something which wasn't planned out.

I told my friend how extremely proud of him I was, and how he had been a role model to me in so many different areas. I explained how he was the single most important friendship that helped me overcome the most difficult time of my life - my divorce. I confessed how the way he handled his own adversity with his positive attitude and actions provided an example to me on how I should respond to adversity when I was at the abysmal point of my depression. I expressed my love for him as a brother, and shared my admiration of the integrity he always carried with him. I praised him for the way he loved God through all circumstances. Finally, I told him that he would never be forgotten, and that his legacy would be carried on by me and so many others. After that statement, he awoke with happiness, but mostly, curiosity in his eyes when he looked at me. I shared that his story would not end with death, but instead would impact strangers he never knew, because I was going to write his story in this book and make sure that no one ever forgot the man that Phil Taylor was during his time here on Earth. His lips pressed together, and his cheek muscles stretched into a smile. He looked to have a sense of peace that overcame him before he fell back out of consciousness.

More family and friends entered the house to say their goodbyes to Phil. We woke him when new visitors arrived, and when friends called on the phone. Sometimes, he would stay awake long enough for us to share what friends had sent in their goodbye messages in text message to our cell phones. With each passing hour, he spent more time sleeping, and less time using his energy to try to interact with us. He was fading quickly.

One of the phone calls that we made sure that he stayed awake the entire time for was from Head Coach Gary Patterson (Coach P), and Offensive Coach Rusty Burns of the TCU football coaching staff. Phil focused intently on the conversation when he heard Coach P's voice on the other end of the phone line. Coach P and Coach Burns told him that he would always be a part of the Horned Frog family, and that he would never be forgotten. They told him that they wished they had more players on the team that had his work ethic and dedication. They shared that he was a role model for others, and that they were proud of the fight against cancer he displayed the past two years. Finally, they said that the Horned Frogs would honor him by placing a sticker with his initials and his number, thirty-five, on the back of each player's helmet for their upcoming game that weekend against, no other than, Iowa State University. He was deeply moved by this display of respect and honor.

He responded with, "Thank you Coach. It means so much to me that you would call me and do that for me." The conversation ended with a sincere goodbye. He smiled for a long time, like he had just scored the game-winning touchdown, before he fell back asleep. Myra smiled with pride for her boy as tears rolled down her face.

An hour later, Myra, and my friends; Marissa, Cobie, Rob, and Danny, all circled around Phil to put our hands on him, and join his pastor in prayer who was in the circle with us, too. After the pastor finished his prayer, he asked us to join him in saying the "Our Father" prayer that Jesus had demonstrated to his disciples when He taught them how they should pray to God. We all bowed our heads and recited the prayer in unison. A few sentences into the historic prayer, I lifted my head up, opened my eyes, and felt a grand smile that will never be matched in intensity again. Phil, who had been sleeping for the past forty-five minutes, sat up as much as he could, and began to join in prayer with us. It took a tremendous amount of effort to recite it, and yet he was able to recite a few sentences in the prayer in unison with us before he faded back to sleep.

That prayer moment will be ingrained in my mind forever; that epitomized the character of Phil Taylor. He fought until the very end, and even though he knew his time on Earth would end soon, he still desired to praise God in his last moments. He wasn't upset about his physical body's deterioration, and the pain it caused him. He wasn't resentful that he was only given twenty-five years to live. He wasn't filled with doubt about his faith in Jesus' redeeming love for him. The man fought for what he believed in until the very end. I've never been more proud of a friend or family member than I was of him during that prayer.

The clock hands continued to tick, and we all continued to think, pray, and wait, not knowing if one of his deep inhales would be his last. We kept telling him to hang onto life, because he had one more friend to see. His old college roommate, Casmir, was flying back from San Diego, California, and he was on a flight headed straight to Dallas. Casmir experienced some flight delays, and when he finally landed in Dallas with his wife, they experienced luggage delays and issues with their mode of transportation to Mike and Sheri's house. We hoped that Casmir would make it in time, and we encouraged Phil to hold on a little longer. Myra sat by his side, and read scripture over him while all other members paced back-and-forth in the living room.

Finally, around 11:00 pm, Casmir walked through the front door. Phil opened his eyes and smiled when he saw Casmir. Phil was able to say in a very low and coarse voice, "Thank you for coming. It means a lot to me." All friends and family members that he expected to see before he passed were finally in one room and sharing our favorite stories of him. We laughed. We cried. We held close to each other as long as we could.

When the clock struck midnight, it was time to leave, and to allow Myra to spend time with Phil in privacy. I gave him one last hug and told him that I loved him. He awoke, looked at me in the eyes, put his palm against my cheek, and didn't say anything. He didn't have to. I already knew that I would see him again in heaven.

Phil passed away in the early hours of the morning on September 25, 2018. He was twenty-five years old.

The Underdog

Phil Taylor lived every single day with integrity. He loved everyone and was beloved by all. He was a class act and the best man that I have ever known.

I encourage you to fight like Phil if you are fighting cancer yourself, going through an unwanted divorce, in severe financial debt, burned, rebounding from a devastating athletic injury, wrongly accused, persecuted due to your skin color or beliefs, bullied, rejected, abused, mocked, an amputee, an addict, lost a child, overweight, trying to break a record, insecure, misunderstood, or trying to change the world. He was an underdog from the beginning of his diagnosis, but he never gave up even in his last hours. We have no excuse to give up either.

"It's a mind game. It's absolutely a mind game. Everyone who goes through this is going to have physical side effects that are very tough to handle, but it's all about their mindset on how they approach it. They have to stay with a positive mindset. They are going to have their moments of doubt, of frustration, and of sadness, and that's okay. They need to find a way to have those emotions cleared out of their system and then go back to being themselves. One thing that I've tried to do is to not let this define me. I don't let this control who I am. My smile is my best weapon."

None of the episodes in the previous chapters are ranked by any criteria, but Phil's story is my favorite, and the one that I cherish the most. His response throughout those years has completely changed countless lives, but none that I can speak of more than mine. When I was depressed and an emotional wreck, he was a solid rock of reason, a patient friend to listen to me spill my heart out when I was crying or pissed off, and he was a Christian man I looked to who led by example, even in the midst of his own mental and emotional battles when he was first diagnosed with cancer at the same time. He was a model for me on how to respond to adversity in my life and that can be summed up with, "Trust God and never stop fighting for what you believe in."

I've learned to accept past heartbreaks, failures, and tribulations as what they are, and shift my perspective to a different level that is not magnified by the immediate pain. We are informed in this world that not everything will be good, but thanks be to God that He can bring good out of any situation.

Phil demonstrated the underdog spirit in an entirely different way for me. He taught me to never stop fighting for something that matters to me even if the world says I have a slim to zero chance of being successful. His courage, fighting spirit, and unwavering faith provided a constant reminder to me of how I should react to all forms of adversity. His example gave me the courage to regain my fighting spirit. His story gave me the hope that somehow, someway, there will be good that comes out of each of our situations. He showed me what an unending selfless devotion to God and to his loved ones really looks like. Witnessing Phil pursue Jesus with his entire heart while undergoing devastating chemotherapy treatments, having multiple surgeries, and frequent emergency trips to the hospital was nothing short of a miracle. In the end, he beat cancer because he didn't let this wicked disease derail him from his faith in a greater purpose, which proved his genuine character, and helped all of his friends and family see what true faith is all about.

I pray that one day I will be the husband that he would have been. I pray that one day I will be the father that he would have been. I pray that every day I strive to become the Christian man that he was. It would be the highest honor that I could attain.

"Who am I to question the plan God has for me? If twenty-five-years is all that I get to have on this earth, then I would like to think that I have had the most awesome twenty-five years possible."

Rest in peace brother. You fought the good fight, and finished the race. You will always be remembered and will never be forgotten.

The next time that you face the hard blow of adversity, take it on the chin, and fight like Phil.

James 1: 2-4 (NIV) – "Consider it pure joy my brothers and sisters whenever you face trials of many kinds, because you know the testing of your faith produces perseverance. Let perseverance finish its work so that you may be mature and complete, not lacking anything."

Acknowledgements

I WOULD LIKE to thank My Savior, Jesus Christ, for all that He has given me, especially the opportunity to share stories that inspire people and give them hope. I am blessed beyond all measure. All glory goes to Him.

Thank you to all forty guests that I had on Underdog Podcast during the first season. All of the guests were incredible, and I learned a valuable lesson from each interview. I look forward to strengthening my friendship with each of you as time moves forward. I highly encourage every reader to listen to all of the episodes.

Thank you to all of my family members and friends that have supported me, encouraged me, and loved me throughout my life. There are too many people to name, but you know who you are.

Thank you to my incredible editor, Curt Locklear. He stayed patient with me during my first book project, even though I have a degree in biology and do not have any writing experience. He provided clear, honest, and concise edit suggestions and helped me navigate through the publishing process. He was not only a great editor, but he became a friend as well, which is what I appreciate the most.

Lastly, thank you to my dear friend, Phil Taylor, who inspired me to write this book. You taught me to never stop fighting for what I believe in. I will carry that with me as long as I live.

Underdog Podcast Episode Archive

Episodes 1-40

ALL EPISODES ARE available on multiple podcast platforms such as Apple Podcasts, Google Play, Stitcher, Spotify and Soundcloud. The episodes, and additional content, are available on www.underdogpc.com

1. **Phil Taylor** – *November 28, 2017*
   a. A former college football player who discussed his outlook on fighting colon cancer, his maintaining optimism, and why he chose to have faith in God no matter the outcome of his fight.

2. **James Anderson** – *November 30, 2017*
   a. He quit his job because he felt called to walk the West Coast from the border of Mexico and the United States to the border of Canada and the United States, and he met many interesting characters along the way.

3. **Chris Singleton** – *December 5, 2017*
   a. He forgave the man who murdered his mother due to a racial motive and followed his dreams to become a professional baseball player.

4. **Alexis Teichmiller** – *December 12, 2017*
   a. A 25-year-old entrepreneur who was born in the cornfields of Illinois and found her way to the spotlight in Nashville, Tennessee. She is the host of the podcast, "The Laptop Lifestyle."

5. **Mason Wells** – *December 19, 2017*
   a. A Navy sailor who was in the vicinity of three separate terrorist attacks in three different countries and survived after sustaining injuries from one of the bombings.

6. **Matt Lindland** – *December 26, 2017*
   a. The 2000 Olympic Silver Medalist in Wrestling for the United States and former number 1 UFC fighter in the world.

7. **Iram Leon** – *January 9, 2018*
   a. The man who has won multiple marathons while battling brain cancer simultaneously.

8. **Danny Kolzow** – *January 16, 2018*
   a. He was in urgent need of a kidney transplant before he found a donor in an unlikely way just before he was scheduled to begin dialysis.

9. **Elisabeth Chauncey** – *January 23, 2018*
   a. She suffered severe burn injuries in an accident, yet completed the World Race, which requires the completion of missionary work in 12 countries in 12 months, and she signed up for this trip before she could walk again.

10. **Richard Overton** – *January 30, 2018*
    a. He was America's oldest veteran at 112 years old (the interview took place when he was 111) before he passed away in December 2018, and we discuss some of the fun memories he had during his long, successful life.

11. **Kim Overton** – *February 13, 2018*
    a. The founder of "SPIbelt". She shares her journey to international success, how she rebounded from

losing money at first, and gives advice to other young entrepreneurs.

12. Tori Murden McClure *– February 20, 2018*
  a. The first woman to row across the Atlantic Ocean, the first woman to ski across the South Pole, a close friend of the late Muhammad Ali, and the President of Spalding University.

13. Michael Morton *– February 27, 2018*
  a. He was found guilty for his wife's murder, and spent nearly twenty-five years in prison before previously hidden evidence confirmed he was innocent which brought about his exoneration. He also shares his encounter with God behind bars.

14. Dre Murray *– March 6, 2018*
  a. A Houston-born rapper who evaded a life filled with crime and drugs that surrounded him and found his way to the top of the iTunes charts by staying true to himself and his beliefs.

15. Jessica Phillips *– March 13, 2018*
  a. A loving mother who lost her daughter, Brooke, to cancer when she was four years old, and created the organization, "B.I.G. Love" in Brooke's memory to help other children cancer patients and their families.

16. Alex Sheen *– March 20, 2018*
  a. The founder of "Because I Said I Would," which is a non-profit organization that encourages others to keep their promises, no matter what.

17. Rock Thomas *– March 27, 2018*
  a. A multi-millionaire, real estate mogul, and best-selling author that began life as a poor farm boy in Canada.

18. Carol Decker *– April 3, 2018*
  a. A mother who relearned how to live life to the fullest after she lost some of her limbs to amputations, and

became blind due to the illness, sepsis which she contracted during the delivery of her baby.

19. <u>Orville Rogers</u> – *April 10, 2018*

    a. A former WWII pilot trainer that picked up running at 50 years old and broke many world records on the path to become the fastest 100-year-old to ever live.

20. <u>Sophia Danenberg</u> – *April 17, 2018*

    a. The first African-American woman, and the first black woman in the world to climb Mount Everest.

21. <u>Shae Brown</u> – *April 24, 2018*

    a. She beat cancer twice, received a heart transplant, and then she ran the Chicago Marathon side-by-side with her donor's father.

22. <u>Matt Pearce</u> – *May 1, 2018*

    a. A Fort Worth Police Officer who was shot multiple times during the pursuit of a wanted criminal and cheated death by persevering through a long recovery.

23. <u>Christy Wise</u> – *May 8, 2018*

    a. The sixth Air Force pilot, and the first woman ever, to return to the sky as an amputee. She is also the founder of "One Leg Up On Life" which provides prostheses to adults and children in Haiti.

24. <u>Dr. Kenneth Cooper</u> – *May 15, 2018*

    a. The man who coined the term "aerobics" and pioneered the fitness revolution within healthcare.

25. <u>James Sides</u> – *May 22, 2018*

    a. A former marine who served in Afghanistan and lost his right hand and the vision in his left eye when a bomb exploded near him. He still found a way to serve his country and represented the United States in the 2018 Paralympic Games as a member of the United States snowboarding team.

26. Michael Vaudreuil – *June 12, 2018*
   a. A loving husband who lost everything, including his job, in the 2008 recession, and became a janitor at a local university. He earned his degree over eight years by taking classes during the day, and cleaning the classroom's floors by night before he became a successful engineer.

27. Harry Patten – *June 19, 2018*
   a. The largest and foremost buyer and seller of rural and undeveloped land in the United States who came from a poor family.

28. Jon Vroman – *June 26, 2018*
   a. The founder of the "Front Row Foundation" which is a charity that creates front row experiences for people with terminal illnesses. He began this organization by completing a double marathon to kick-start the funding for its mission.

29. Kelubia Mabatah – *July 3, 2018*
   a. A former collegiate tennis player who was attacked and brutally beaten by a group of men for an unknown reason. They left Kelubia for dead, but he survived. He lost his ability to talk and his ability to walk, but relearned how to do both through extensive rehab.

30. Carolyn Colleen Bostrack – *July 10, 2018*
   a. She overcame multiple abusive relationships as a child and as an adult, and became a PhD, an author, and a keynote speaker, but most importantly, a terrific mother to her three children.

31. Drew Manning – *July 17, 2018*
   a. A personal trainer who gained seventy plus pounds on purpose from a poor diet over six months, and then reversed course, and lost it all in the following six months. He learned a lot about physical, mental, and emotional adversity on the way, and learned how to empathize with his clients.

32. <u>Kacey Gorringe</u> – *July 24, 2018*
   a. A former heroin addict who was arrested for drug possession, then turned his life around and became a successful real estate entrepreneur.

33. <u>Toni McKinley</u> – *July 31, 2018*
   a. She grew up as a human trafficking victim in childhood. She was able to escape when she was an adult, and she became a counselor to help other child victims of sex trafficking rehabilitate, heal, and leave that evil trade behind.

34. <u>Rob Pope</u> – *August 7, 2018*
   a. The first person ever to retrace Forrest Gump's steps and run across America four times. The route took 422 days to complete, and he ran over 15,000 miles.

35. <u>Shay Eskew</u> – *August 14, 2018*
   a. He was severely burned as a child, and had over thirty-five surgeries to heal his wounds. He was told by doctors that he would most likely never be able to participate in sports again, but he went on to become one of the top Ironmen race competitors in the world.

36. <u>Stephen Moore</u> – *August 21, 2018*
   a. He lost his leg in a motorcycle accident, but that didn't stop him from winning Strongman Competitions, and weightlifting competitions, as an amputee among competitors that were not amputees.

37. <u>Kyle Oxford</u> – *August 28, 2018*
   a. He fought for his marriage, even though his ex-wife continued to struggle with infidelity. Depression and alcohol use were some of the poor decisions he made after his divorce, but he was restored with faith and love when he met a new woman and remarried.

38. <u>Dr. Geoff Tabin</u> – *September 4, 2018*
   a. One of the co-founders of the "Himalayan Cataract Project" which is an organization that is striving to

end all unnecessary blindness throughout the world. He is also the fourth person ever to climb the tallest mountain on all seven continents.

39. Tommy Green – *September 11, 2018*

    a. The leader of the hardcore rock band, Sleeping Giant. He overcame an abusive father as a child. Many of the poor decisions that he made when he was a young adult was due to that pain. However, he eventually became the virtuous rock star that he is today.

40. Rey Ybarra – *September 18, 2018*

    a. He interviewed and published a book about the lives of many famous entrepreneurs who won on TV's hit show, "Shark Tank." He was able to complete this book, which happened to be his first, even though he has been suffering from the daily debilitating pain of Rheumatoid Arthritis for the past two decades.

CPSIA information can be obtained
at www.ICGtesting.com
Printed in the USA
FSHW021256300119
55364FS